Industrial Innovation in the United Kingdom, Canada and the United States

by Kerry Schott

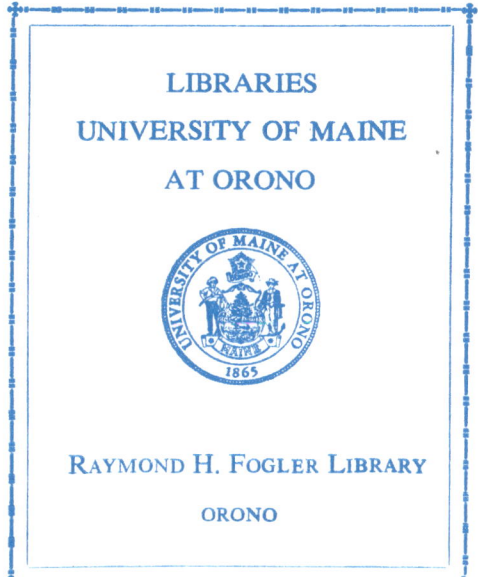

BRITISH-NORTH AMERICAN COMMITTEE

Sponsored by
British-North American Research Association (UK)
NPA (USA)
C. D. Howe Institute (Canada)

© British-North American Committee 1981
Short quotations with appropriate credit permissible

ISBN 0-902594-39-7

Published by the British-North American Committee
Printed and bound in the United Kingdom by
Contemprint Limited, London, England.

July 1981

Contents

The British-North American Committee........................INSIDE FRONT COVER

Statement by the British-North American Committee
to Accompany the Report.. v

Members of the Committee Signing the Statement v

Author's Preface ix

INDUSTRIAL INNOVATION IN THE UNITED KINGDOM, CANADA AND THE UNITED STATES
by Kerry Schott

Introduction.. 1

I. Indicators of Innovation in the United Kingdom, Canada and the United States
    A. National Research and Development Expenditures 5
    B. The Number of Scientists and Engineers
       Employed on R & D.. 15
    C. Patent Applications.. 18
    D. Technology Transfers 20
    E. Summary.. 22

II. Innovation and the Economy
    A. Innovation, Productivity and Growth 25
    B. Innovation, Investment and Employment 31
    C. Innovation and Trade... 37
    D. Summary.. 42

III. The Economy and Innovation
    A. The Current Economic Climate... 45
    B. The Determinants of Innovation... 46
       1. Economic Determinants... 46
       2. Institutional Factors... 52
    C. The Influence of the Government... 54
    D. Summary.. 62

IV. Policy Issues 63

Members of the British-North American Committee........................... x

Sponsoring Organizations.. xvi

Publications of the British-North American Committee...INSIDE BACK COVER

List of Tables

		Page
Table 1	Trends in Expenditure on R & D as a Percentage of GNP in the United Kingdom, Canada and the United States	5
Table 2	R & D as a Precentage of GNP, 1969, 1975 & 1978 and Total R & D Expenditure 1975	6
Table 3	Industrial R & D Expenditure on Basic Research as a Percentage of Total Industrial R & D, 1967, 1971 & 1975	7
Table 4	Index of Real Expenditure on R & D Performed in Higher Education, 1967-1975	8
Table 5	Industrial R & D Expenditure in the United Kingdom, 1975	12
Table 6	Industrial R & D Expenditure in the United States, 1977	13
Table 7	Industrial R & D Expenditure in Canadian Industry, 1974	14
Table 8	Scientists & Engineers Engaged on UK Industrial R & D, December 1975	16
Table 9	R & D Scientists & Engineers Employed in US Industry, January 1978	17
Table 10	Personnel Engaged in R & D in Industry in Canada, 1974	17
Table 11	Patent Applications Filed, 1970-76 in Selected OECD Countries	19
Table 12	Payments and Receipts by Canadian Firms for Industrial Technology	21
Table 13	Net US Receipt of Royalties and Licensing Fees	21
Table 14	Index of Real GDP per Employee, Selected Countries	27
Table 15	Sources of Growth of National Income per Employee, in the Non-residential Business Sector in the United States, 1948-73, 1973-76	29
Table 16	Percentage of Labour Force Unemployed 1974-1978	33
Table 17	Share in the Value of Exports of Manufacturers, 1950-1979	38
Table 18	Unit Labour Costs in Manufacturing, 1950-1977	40
Table 19	Hourly Compensation of Production Workers in Manufacturing, 1960-1977	41
Table 20	The Different Background of Management in Selected Countries	50
Table 21	Estimated Innovation Rate in Major Innovations per R & D Dollar	53
Table 22	Deployment of Government Financed Expenditure on R & D in Selected Countries 1975	56

List of Figures

Figure 1	Industry as a Source of Funds for Industrial R & D, 1973	9
Figure 2	Trends in Real Industry Financed R & D Expenditure	10
Figure 3	R & D Scientists/Engineers per 10,000 of the Labour Force by Country, 1965-1975	15
Figure 4	Investment and Productivity, Selected Countries, 1960-1976	32
Figure 5	Summary of the Quantitative and Qualitative Impacts of Technical Change on Employment in a Number of Industries	34

Statement of the British-North American Committee to Accompany the Report

Discussion among members of the British-North American Committee has revealed considerable concern at the fact that the proportion of Gross National Product devoted to industrial research and development in the United Kingdom, Canada and the United States has been falling both relatively and absolutely. It is argued that various disincentives in the three Western countries have resulted in lower R & D investment. Members have also been particularly puzzled at the apparent slowness to adopt innovations for products and processes for the majority of industries in the three countries. To help to understand why this should be, the British-North American Committee asked Dr. Kerry Schott, lecturer in economics at the Department of Political Economy, University College, London to review what is known about the process of innovation, what affects it and what steps might be taken by governments and businesses to stimulate more of it.

This is her report; we commend it to a wider audience both as a useful summary of the complexities of the topic and a guide to constructive thinking about it.

The Committee expects to continue working on this subject which it considers to be of the utmost importance to the future of economic activity in our respective nations.

Members of the Committee Signing the Statement

R. W. ADAM
A Managing Director,
The British Petroleum Company Limited

JOSEPH E. BAIRD
Pacific Palisades, California

ROBERT A. BANDEEN
President and Chief Executive Officer,
Canadian National

SIR DONALD BARRON
Trustee,
The Joseph Rowntree Memorial Trust

CARL E. BEIGIE
President,
C. D. Howe Institute

MICHEL BELANGER
President and Chief Executive Officer,
National Bank of Canada

JOHN F. BOOKOUT
President and Chief Executive Officer,
Shell Oil Company

THORNTON F. BRADSHAW
President,
Atlantic Richfield Company

SIR GEORGE BURTON
Chairman,
Fisons Limited

SIR RICHARD BUTLER
President,
National Farmers' Union

Committee Signers

VISCOUNT CALDECOTE
Chairman, Delta Metal Company and
Chairman, Finance for Industry

SIR CHARLES CARTER
Chairman of Research and Management
Committee, Policy Studies Institute

HAROLD VAN B. CLEVELAND
Vice President,
Citibank, N.A.

JAMES W. DAVANT
Chairman of the Board,
Paine Webber Incorporated

RALPH P. DAVIDSON
Chairman,
Time Incorporated

DIRK DE BRUYNE
Managing Director,
Royal Dutch/Shell Group of Companies

A. H. A. DIBBS
Deputy Chairman,
National Westminster Bank Limited

SIR RICHARD DOBSON
Richmond, Surrey

WILLIAM H. DONALDSON
Chairman and Chief Executive,
Donaldson Enterprises Inc.

SIR ALASTAIR DOWN
Chairman,
Burmah Oil Company

GEOFFREY DRAIN
General Secretary,
National Association of Local Government
Officers

JOHN DU CANE
Chairman and Chief Executive,
Selection Trust Limited

TERRY DUFFY
President,
Amalgmated Union of Engineering Workers

GERRY EASTWOOD
General Secretary,
Association of Patternmakers and
Allied Craftsmen

HARRY E. EKBLOM
Chairman and Chief Execurive Officer,
European American Bancorp

J. K. FINLAYSON
President,
The Royal Bank of Canada

GLENN FLATEN
President,
Canadian Federation of Agriculture

SIR ALASTAIR FRAME
Chief Executive,
Rio-Tinto Zinc Corporation

RICHARD W. FOXEN
Corporate Vice President-International,
Rockwell International Corp.

ROBERT R. FREDERICK
Executive Vice President,
International Sector,
General Electric Company

THEODORE GEIGER
Distinguished Research Professor of
Intersocietal Relations School of Foreign
Service, Georgetown University

MALCOLM GLENN
Executive Vice President,
Reed Holdings Incorporated

GEORGE GOYDER
British Secretary,
BNAC

JOHN H. HALE
Executive Vice President,
Alcan Aluminium Limited

HON. HENRY HANKEY
Westerham, Kent

FRED L. HARTLEY
Chairman and President,
Union Oil Company of California

G. R. HEFFERNAN
President,
Co-Steel International Ltd.

ROBERT HENDERSON
Chairman,
Kleinwort Benson Ltd.

TOM JACKSON
General Secretary,
Union of Communication Workers

JOHN V. JAMES
Chairman of the Board,
President and Chief Executive Officer,
Dresser Industries, Inc.

GEORGE S. JOHNSTON
President,
Scudder, Stevens & Clark

Committee Signers

JOSEPH D. KEENAN
President,
Union Label and Service Trades Department,
AFL-CIO

TOM KILLEFER
Chairman of the Board and Chief Executive Officer,
United States Trust Company of New York

CURTIS M. KLAERNER
President and Chief Operating Officer,
Commonwealth Oil Refining Company

H. U. A. LAMBERT
Chairman,
Barclays Bank International Ltd.

HERBERT H. LANK
Honorary Director,
Du Pont Canada Inc.

WILLIAM A. LIFFERS
Vice Chairman,
American Cyanamid Company

FRANKLIN A. LINDSAY
Chairman,
Itek Corporation

SIR PETER MACADAM
Chairman,
B.A.T. Industries Ltd.

CARGILL MacMILLAN, JR.
Senior Vice President,
Cargill Inc.

JOHN D. MACOMBER
Chairman,
Celanese Corporation

J. P. MANN
Deputy Chairman,
United Biscuits (Holdings) Ltd.

A. B. MARSHALL
Chairman,
Bestobell Ltd.

WILLIAM J. McDONOUGH
Chairman,
Asset and Liability Management Committee,
The First National Bank of Chicago, Chicago

DONALD E. MEADS
Chairman and President,
Carver Associates

SIR PATRICK MEANEY
Group Managing Director,
Thomas Tilling Limited

SIR PETER MENZIES
Welwyn, Hertfordshire

JOHN MILLER
Vice Chairman, and Acting President,
National Planning Association

DEREK F. MITCHELL
Chairman and Chief Executive Officer,
BP Canada Limited.

ALLEN E. MURRAY
President of Marketing and Refining Division,
Mobil Oil Corporation

KENNETH D. NADEN
President,
National Council of Farmer Cooperatives

WILLIAM S. OGDEN
Vice Chairman,
The Chase Manhattan Bank, N.A.

BROUGHTON PIPKIN
Stow-on-the-Wold, Glouc.

SIR RICHARD POWELL
Hill Samuel Group Ltd.

ALFRED POWIS
Chairman and President,
Noranda Mines Limited

LOUIS PUTZE
Consultant,
Rockwell International Corp.

BEN ROBERTS
Professor of Industrial Relations,
London School of Economics

HAROLD B. ROSE
Group Economic Advisor,
Barclays Bank Limited

DAVID SAINSBURY
Director of Finance,
J. Sainsbury Ltd.

WILLIAM SALOMON
Limited Partner and Honorary Member of the Executive Committee,
Salomon Brothers

A. C. I. SAMUEL
Handcross, Sussex

NATHANIEL SAMUELS
Chairman,
Advisory Board Lehman Brothers Kuhn Loeb Inc., and
Chairman,
Olivetti Corporation

SIR FRANCIS SANDILANDS
Chairman,
Commercial Union Assurance Company, Ltd.

HON. MAURICE SAUVE
Executive Vice President,
Administrative and Public Affairs,
Consolidated Bathurst Inc.

PETER F. SCOTT
President,
Provincial Insurance Company, Ltd.

ROBERT C. SEAMANS, JR.
Massachusetts Institute of Technology

LORD SEEBOHM
Dedham, Essex

THE EARL OF SELKIRK
President,
Royal Central Asian Society

JACOB SHEINKMAN
Secretary-Treasurer,
Amalgamated Clothing & Textile Workers'
Union

LORD SHERFIELD
Chairman,
Raytheon Europe International Company

R. MICHAEL SHIELDS
Managing Director,
Associated Newspapers Group Ltd.

GEORGE L. SHINN
Chairman and Chief Executive Officer,
The First Boston Corporation

GEORGE SHULTZ
Vice-Chairman,
Bechtel Group of Companies

GORDON R. SIMPSON
Chairman,
General Accident Fire and Life Assurance
Corporation Ltd.

SIR ROY SISSON
Chairman,
Smiths Industries Limited

ARTHUR J. R. SMITH
Consultant,
Washington, D.C.

SIR LESLIE SMITH
Chairman,
BOC International

E. NORMAN STAUB
Chairman and Chief Executive Officer,
The Northern Trust Company

RALPH I. STRAUS
New York, N.Y.

SIR ROBERT TAYLOR
Deputy Chairman,
Standard Chartered Bank Ltd.

WILLIAM I. M. TURNER, JR.
President and Chief Executive Officer,
Consolidated-Bathurst Inc.

JOHN W. TUTHILL
President,
The Salzburg Seminar
Washington, D.C.

W. O. TWAITS
Toronto, Ontario

MARTHA REDFIELD WALLACE
Director,
The Henry Luce Foundation Inc.

GLENN E. WATTS
President,
Communications Workers of America,
AFL-CIO

WILLIAM WEARLY
Chairman, Executive Committee,
Ingersoll-Rand Company

VISCOUNT WEIR
Vice Chairman,
The Weir Group Limited

FREDERICK B. WHITTEMORE
Managing Director,
Morgan Stanley & Co. Incorporated

SIR ERNEST WOODROOFE
Former Chairman,
Unilever Ltd.

Author's Preface

I am grateful to the British-North American Committee (BNAC) for supporting my work on this topic and for the comments, suggestions and encouragement which I have received from the members. I am particularly grateful to Sir Charles Carter for his comments on various drafts of this paper. Simon Webley and Melanie Walsh, the BNAC staff in London, provided administrative assistance and moral support in preparing for the various BNAC meetings. The Washington office of the BNAC was very helpful in arranging meetings with US government officials and academics with whom I had useful discussions in December 1979. Sperry Lea and Professor Terleckyj were particularly helpful. My thanks to all these people. None of them, nor the BNAC collectively, bears any responsibility for the contents of this paper.

March 1981   Kerry Schott
University College, London

Dr. Kerry Schott *is a lecturer in economics at University College, London. Before joining University College she taught economics at Southampton University, 1976-1978. She was one of several economists on the Australian Government's Priority Review Staff in 1975, and earlier she worked on the development of an econometric model of the Australian economy at the Reserve Bank of Australia. Her interest in innovation began in 1972 at Nuffield College, Oxford and she has published a number of papers on the economics of industrial innovation. In 1980/81 she was a Visiting Lecturer at Princeton University.*

Industrial Innovation in the United Kingdom, Canada and the United States

Introduction

One of the outstanding features of the last decade has been the relatively poor economic performance of the United Kingdom, Canada and the United States. The record for the 1970s in these three countries compares unfavourably with their economic behaviour in the fifties and sixties: living standards have not increased as much, investment rates have been lower, company profit levels have fallen, unemployment has been higher and prices have risen sharply.

These problems have to an extent been shared by all developed countries but some, notably Japan and West Germany, have fared relatively better. International competition from the more successful nations has accentuated the difficulties in Britain and North America with the result that the respective shares of these three countries in the world trade of manufactures has fallen.

These economic problems have now been with us for some time and have been subjected to considerable analysis. In the United States recent attention has concentrated on the causes and consequences of the slowdown in productivity growth; in the United Kingdom and Canada unemployment and the maintenance of living standards in the face of rising prices has been the focus. All these issues are obviously interrelated and connected, either directly or indirectly, with economic growth.

This study concentrates on industrial innovation and the links between it and economic growth. In the recent past, when growth rates were high, it was generally agreed that improving technology was a major determining factor; when growth is slow and economic problems abound, it seems reasonable to give special attention to innovation. To what extent, for example, have the economic problems of Britain and North America been exacerbated by declining innovation activity? Are these three countries doing sufficient innovation to compete effectively in international trade? What effect is the current economic climate having on corporate innovation decisions?

These macroeconomic questions recur throughout this paper. There are no easy answers to them and consequently no quick solutions to the current economic malaise. What does emerge is the circular linkage between innovation and economic performance. The argument runs like this: the relatively poor economic performance of the UK, Canada, and the US inhibits innovation; the declining growth in innovative activity in turn inhibits economic performance. Official statistics indicate that the proportion of national resources devoted to technical innovation in the UK has been falling since 1967 and in Canada and the United States since 1973. This, coupled with low investment activity, has contributed to poor productivity rates and growing unemployment in the face of intense international competition. All this subsequently discourages innovation and a vicious circle becomes apparent.

Chapter I examines the innovative performance of France, West Germany, and Japan, as well as the United States, Canada and the United Kingdom. While there is no single indicator of innovative activity and those used are somewhat crude, all point to the same conclusion: the rate of innovation in Britain and North America is smaller than that of its principal competitors.

The first chapter also discusses the spread of innovation across different industries. It concludes that industry-funded innovation is concentrated in the chemical and electronic sectors particularly in the United Kingdom and the United States but it is also apparent in the other four countries. Government funds for innovation are spread in different ways across the countries examined but the relatively high UK and US defence commitments are obvious in the data.

The implications for the economies of Britain and North America of their relatively smaller innovation rates are explored in Chapter II. The statistics show that productivity growth and investment per person is lower; unemployment rates are higher; shares in world trade are declining; and the increase in wages and salaries paid to employees is also lower.

Chapter III then explores what determines the rate of innovation in an economic climate where uncertainty and lower expected profits prevail. It is suggested that the current decline in innovation is not irrational and indeed is a reasonably predictable response to these conditions.

The final chapter is devoted to examining policies concerned with encouraging innovation. It is argued that an increase in innovative activity will not by itself solve the economic problem: rather it is a vital ingredient in any policy package aimed to achieve economic recovery. The most favourable environment for stimulating innovation would be a regime of stable prices with economic growth. But neither of these goals is likely to be achieved without a marked increase in innovative activity in Britain and North America. Hence the dilemma for the policy maker; he or she must take account of this but at the same time recognise that a policy which simply stimulates technological activity alone will not bring success.

It is necessary at the start to be clear what we mean by the word innovation and to emphasise the complex nature of the subject of this paper. Innovation is a process which is distinctive in each case and hence really defies adequate definition. It covers all that goes on from the beginning of an idea, to an invention, through to the marketing of a new product and the use of a new process. Innovation in fact, continues until the new product or process has been completely introduced into the economy, along with any modifications and improvements. It could be said that innovation begins with an idea and ends with the widespread use of a new product and widespread new process diffusion.

This notion, however, leads to a description of each innovation broken down into stages and thus implies that each innovation has to move through each stage. This is not correct since every innovation is unique and can begin and end in all sorts of ways. One presentation of an industrial innovation might be as follows: a firm seeks to achieve profitable, continuing and expanding sales. The continuity and expansion of sales can come from new product innovations but it can also be achieved by lower unit costs of production via process innovations. Research and development may be needed to introduce the new products and processes but R & D are also feedback activities which when applied, result in design and quality alterations and may lead to increased sales and profit.

The term 'research' in this paper includes basic or fundamental research as well as applied research which is more oriented to specific problem solving. Development is the application of research and embraces product design. Marketing involves not only sales but information feedback from customers and others, to production and research and development. Satisfying the needs of customers (consciously or unconsciously) is the basis of forming product policy; this in turn sets objectives for research. Innovation is a complex process for which no one description is adequate.

I. Indicators of Innovation in the United Kingdom, Canada and the United States

The diverse nature of innovation means that it is impossible to develop any single completely satisfactory measure of innovative activity. A successful industrial innovation with a high level of diffusion is in part the result of existing knowledge, research and development, commercial and technical evaluation, design, production, marketing, sales and subsequent profits.

There are some data which give an indication of the overall trend in innovative activity in the United Kingdom, Canada and the United States, but they relate more to the R & D part of the innovation than other aspects. The most impressive thing about the indicators considered here is that all point to the same general conclusion. Innovation rates in Britain and North America are generally declining and do not compare favourably with other competing countries.

A. NATIONAL RESEARCH AND DEVELOPMENT EXPENDITURE

Total research and development expenditure in the United Kingdom, United States and Canada, as a percentage of gross national product are shown in Table 1. As R & D is only one part of the innovation process, this indicator is at best a rough guide to the states of innovation activity in any country.

Table 1

Trends in Expenditure on R & D as a percentage of GNP in United Kingdom, Canada and the United States

	1963	1967	1971	1975
UNITED KINGDOM				
Total	2.30%*	2.30%	2.10%†	2.10%
Defence	0.79	0.61	0.53	0.62
Other	1.51	1.69	1.57	1.48
CANADA				
Total	1.00	1.20	1.20	1.00
Defence	0.09	0.09	0.06	0.04
Other	0.91	1.11	1.14	0.96
UNITED STATES				
Total	2.90	2.90	2.60	2.30
Defence	1.37	1.10	0.80	0.64
Other	1.53	1.80	1.80	1.66

Source: OECD: *Science & Technology in the New Socio-Economic Context,* 1979
*1964 †1972

In all three countries the R & D/GNP ratio has tended to fall in the decade up to 1975 and in the United Kingdom the decline commenced as far back as 1967. More recent but tentative OECD estimates of this ratio, (in the OECD *Observer*, March 1981), also show that there is no significant change in this trend. The share of R & D expenditure on defence has fallen in the US and Canada but in the UK it increased between 1971 and 1975.

This relative decline in R & D expenditure is not being experienced by all developed countries as Table 2 shows. West Germany, Japan and the USSR for instance, all increased their R & D/GNP over the 1967-1975 period. The relatively low share of R & D expenditure in Canada is also notable in both Tables 1 and 2.

Table 2
R & D as a Percent of GNP, 1969, 1975, 1978 and total R & D expenditure 1975

	1969	1975	1978	Total R & D Expenditure 1975 $ US billion
United Kingdom	2.2%	2.1%	•	$4.6 billion
Canada	1.3	1.0	•	1.7
United States	2.7	2.3	2.2%	35.2
France	1.9	1.8	•	6.0
West Germany	2.0	2.4	2.3	8.8
Japan	1.6	1.9	•	8.8
USSR	3.0	3.7	•	•

Source: OECD, Directorate for Science, Technology & Industry; and USSR estimate from Dr. Robert Campbell, Indiana University.
• Not available.

The money expenditure (in US dollars) on research and development in 1975, shown in the last column in Table 2, indicates the substantial absolute advantage of the United States. Although there has been a decline in the R & D/GNP ratio in the United States, in absolute terms the US effort is still about four times higher than that in Japan and West Germany, seven times higher than that in the United Kingdom and twenty times that in Canada.

Not all total aggregate R & D expenditure is necessarily an input into industrial innovation. The basic research component, however funded, adds to existing knowledge and may increase the likelihood of fundamental discoveries at the initial stage of innovation. The importance of this type of research to industrial innovation is often overlooked and a number of empirical studies on the subject in the United States indicate that access to the results of basic research is an important prerequisite for successful innovation[1]. The share of industrial R & D expenditure devoted to it is shown in Table 3.

Table 3

Industrial R & D Expenditure on Basic Research as a Percentage of Total Industrial R & D 1967, 1971 & 1975

	1967	1971	1975
United Kingdom	3.4%	•	3.3%
Canada	4.7	4.0%	•
United States	3.5	3.4	3.0
France	4.2	3.4	•
West Germany	5.1	7.1	4.7
Japan	10.2	9.1	5.2

Source: OECD, *Science & Technology in the New Socio-Economic Context*, 1979
• Not available.

As basic research is difficult to identify separately from applied research and development, these figures give only a rough indication of how the countries listed compare. Overall the resources devoted to basic research have fallen but the relatively high share of West Germany and Japan is conspicuous. Price and Bass[2] found that access by industry to basic discoveries is enhanced if they themselves participate in fundamental research and this decline in their basic research expenditures is, therefore, of some concern. If continued, it will limit the expertise available for recognising the importance of existing research as well as decreasing the chances of expanding the frontiers of existing knowledge. Industry must do sufficient basic research to enable it at least to recognize the potential importance of scientific advances throughout the whole international world of science. If this is not being done then it will result in an increasing disadvantage in the market-place.

Industry can also gain access to basic discovery through the transfer and acquisition of knowledge at higher education institutions.

---

1 See: Price, W. J. & Bass, C. W., Scientific research in the innovative process, *Science*, Vol. 162, No. 3881. 1969.

2 Ibid.

The trends in real expenditure on R & D undertaken in places of higher education are shown in Table 4. The United Kingdom and the United States have barely increased their effort since 1967 while Japan and Germany have expanded their real expenditure by over 90% and 60% respectively. Proportions of government R & D expenditure allocated to the general advancement of knowledge ranges from 3.9% in the US, 22% in the UK and Canada, to over 50% in Japan and Germany[3]. These OECD figures are adjusted for comparisons between countries but the US figure seems very low and hence some caution should be exercised in interpreting these data.

Table 4
Index of Real Expenditure on R & D Performed in Higher Education 1967-75
(1967 = 100)

	1967	1970	1975
United Kingdom	100	97	108
Canada	100	124	123
United States	100	103	106
West Germany	100	141	162
Japan	100	139	193
France	100	119	131

Source: OECD, *Science & Technology in the New Socio-Economic Context,* 1979

While basic research and R & D in higher education institutions may ultimately encourage industrial innovation, the major component of industrial R & D is that financed by industry itself. As one would expect, the proportion varies considerably between countries and industries, as shown in Figure 1. This indicates that in both West Germany and Japan almost 80% and 93% respectively of all industrial R & D is paid for by industrial firms. These percentages compare to 58% industry-funded industrial R & D in the UK and 61% in the US. In both the United Kingdom and Canada, industry's share of funding of industrial R & D has been fairly steady during the 1960's and 1970's. However, in the United States industry's share of funding has risen from 42% in 1960 to 65% in 1977[4]. This rise however, largely reflects federal government

---

[3] OECD, *Science & Technology in the New Socio-Economic Context,* 1979.
[4] National Science Foundation, *National Patterns of R & D Resources,* Washington D.C., 1976

cut-backs in R & D funding in the US, particularly in defence and, especially, space programmes.

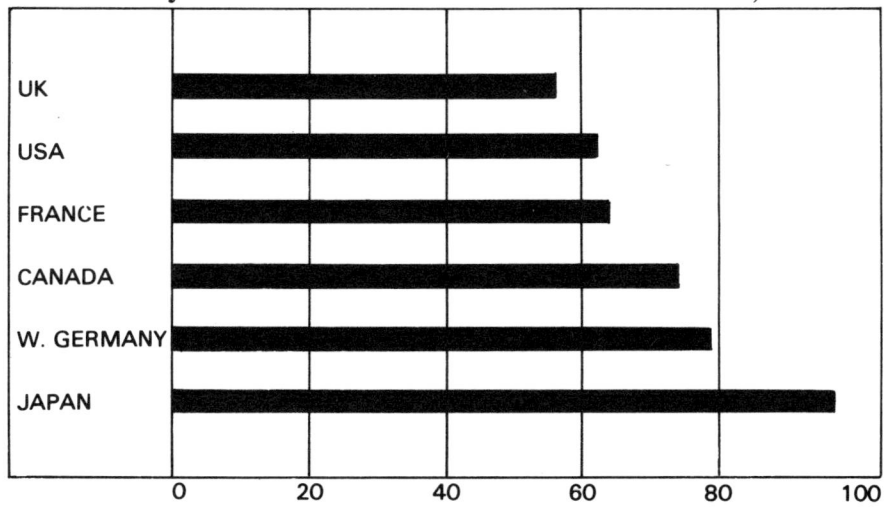

Figure 1
Industry as a Source of Funds for Industrial R & D, 1973

PERCENTAGE FUNDED BY INDUSTRY

Source: OECD, *Statistics Canada,* CSO, *Economic Trends,* July 1979

A high proportion of industrial R & D funded by governments is directed to defence, and other non-economic objectives, and hence may not contribute directly to economic performance. This is particularly important in the UK and the US where almost 50% of government R & D expenditure is directly defence oriented. In Canada, defence R & D is only 6.1% of total government R & D expenditures and in Japan and West Germany defence R & D is 2.2% and 11.1% respectively[5].

The relative success of the economies of Japan and West Germany then, may be related to the high share of industry-funded industrial R & D expenditure in the total. This is not to deny that economic spin-offs from government industrial R & D projects, aimed at non-economic objectives, are possible. But available evidence suggests that overall, the positive economic impact of these spin-offs is small. The National Aeronautics and Space Administration (NASA) in the United States is currently arguing, in a bid to justify funding, that the economic benefits

---

5   OECD, Directorate for Science, Technology & Industry.

of its research programme are large. The cost-benefit analysis on which this argument rests is at best tentative[6], most innovations that result from spin-offs of this kind could have been more economically achieved if the R & D had been initially aimed at the commercial innovation and not at some defence or space objective.

Real trends in industry-financed R & D are shown in Figure 2. The index numbers on which this chart is based are derived from industry-funded R & D expenditure data that are deflated by the relevant GNP price deflator. This attempt to adjust for cost and price changes in R & D expenditure probably underestimates the cost increases in R & D inputs, since R & D is more labour intensive than most components of the GNP and labour costs have increased more rapidly than other R & D costs in most countries.

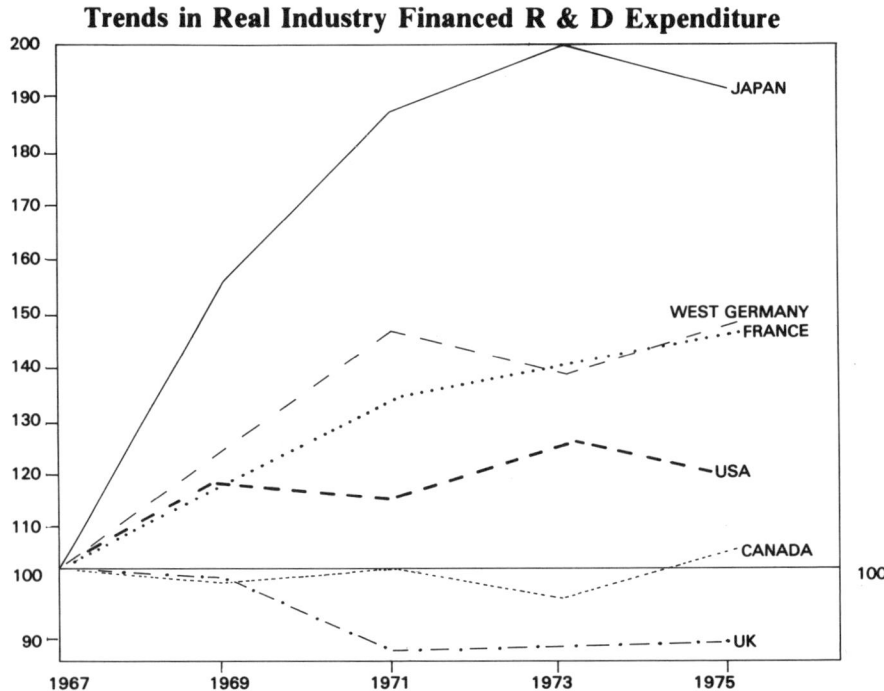

Figure 2
Trends in Real Industry Financed R & D Expenditure

Source: OECD, *Science & Technology in the New Socio-Economic Context*, 1979.

---

6 Mathematica Inc., *Quantifying the Benefits to the National Economy from Secondary Applications of NASA Technology*, 1975.

The outstanding feature of the trends shown in Figure 2 is the poor performance of the United Kingdom compared with that of Japan, which has increased real industry-financed R & D by almost 100%, and West Germany and France where the real increases have been about 35%. In the United States the figure is low at 10%, while in Canada there has been very little change at all between 1967 and 1975. The United Kingdom, Canada and the United States do not compare favourably with West Germany, France or Japan as far as real industry-financed R & D expenditures are concerned, although in all countries the pace of real growth in Industrial R & D expenditures has slackened since the early 1970's.

Over 95% of all industrial R & D is performed in manufacturing industry irrespective of the country. In the United Kingdom the industrial R & D effort is heavily concentrated. That financed by industry occurs mainly in the chemical and electrical engineering industries which together account for 50% of industry-funded R & D. Within electrical engineering the major R & D effort is in electronics and communication including the computer industry. Government funds for industrial R & D are even more highly concentrated; in the UK in 1975 94% went to the electrical engineering (including electronics) (35%) and aerospace industries (59%).

While the total decline in resources devoted to R & D in the UK has affected all sectors of industry, the concentration of industrial R & D expenditure in aerospace, chemicals and electrical engineering has intensified. Basic metals, mechanical engineering and other manufacturing industries have been affected by a shift away from these relatively low research active sectors. The R & D expenditure pattern in UK industry in 1975 is shown in Table 5. The decline in industrial R & D activity in the UK is thus most especially a decline in the effort in chemicals, electrical engineering, including electronics, aerospace and communications, other sectors of UK industry are not research intensive.

The situation in the United States is somewhat different. The relative decline in R & D activity has been more evenly spread across all sectors of industry and the concentration of industrial R & D in a few industries is not so strong as in the United Kingdom. Government funded industrial R & D is, like the UK, heavily concentrated in aerospace (55%) and the electrical and electronics industries (30%).

Industry-funded R & D is concentrated in the electrical and electronics industry, chemical, machinery and in other transport

Table 5
Industrial R & D Expenditure in the United Kingdom, 1975
(millions of pounds)

	Total	Funds from Private Industry	Funds from Public Corporations	Funds from Government
MANUFACTURING: TOTAL	£1,302m	£800m	£115m	£408m
Chemical & allied products (total)	251	236	7	7
Pharmaceuticals	81	81	0	0
Paint	7	7	0	0
Synthetic rubber, resins & plastic	27	26	0	0
Other chemical	136	121	7	7
Mechanical engineering (total)	104	66	33	5
Electrical engineering (total)	352	167	45	140
Electronics & communication	279	113	36	130
Electrical machinery	34	20	7	6
Insulated wire & cables	11	9	2	0
Domestic appliances	6	} 24	} 0	} 3
Miscellaneous electrical goods	21			
Motor vehicles	88	87	0	1
Aerospace	292	52	0	240
Textiles & man-made fibres	26	26	0	0
All other manufacturing	189	166	30	4
NON-MANUFACTURING	49	16	27	6
Total product groups	1352	796	142	414
Per cent	100%	58.9%	10.5%	30.6%

Source: Central Statistical Office, *Economic Trends*, July 1979 (Figures may not sum exactly due to rounding)

industries (excluding aerospace). Research and development expenditures in US industry for 1977 are shown in Table 6.

Table 6
Industrial R & D Expenditure in the United States, 1977
(millions of US dollars)

	Total	Funds from	
		Industry	Government
TOTAL: ALL INDUSTRY	$29,907m	$19,362m	$10,545m
Chemical & allied products	3,267	2,973	294
Machinery	3,970	3,393	577
Electrical & communication	5,952	3,256	2,696
Transportation (including aerospace)	10,497	4,520	5,977
Professional & scientific instruments	1,405	1,249	156
All other industry	4,816	3,971	845

Source: National Science Foundation, *R & D in Industry,* 1977, Washington D.C.

In Canada the concentration of the research effort is similar except that there is less emphasis on aerospace. The electrical, chemical, machinery and transportation industries account for 75% of industry-funded R & D. The expenditure on R & D in all other sectors of Canadian industry is not as concentrated. In machinery and transportation equipment about 36% of industrial R & D is funded by the government but in other sectors of industry the share of government funding is noticeably more modest. Industrial R & D expenditure for work performed in Canadian industry in 1974 is shown in Table 7 (overleaf).

West Germany and Japan also concentrate their industrial R & D in the electrical (including electronics), chemical and machinery industries but the transport industry, excluding aerospace, is also heavily research oriented; the basic metal industries are also important in Japan.

There are several striking features that emerge from the research and development expenditure data in the United Kingdom, Canada and the United States. The first is the relatively low rate of growth of R & D activity in all three countries as compared to West Germany and Japan. The United Kingdom is particularly behind, and Canada has a notably low share of R & D expenditure to gross national product.

Table 7
R & D Expenditure in Canadian Industry, 1974
(millions of Canadian dollars)

	Total	Funds from		
		Industry	Federal Government	Other
TOTAL INDUSTRY:	C$564.7m	C$392.1m	C$84.2m	C$88.4m
Mines & wells	28.6	22.6	1.8	4.2
Chemical based	127.8	109.7	7.3	10.8
Wood based	27.1	15.2	2.6	9.3
Metals	55.2	48.6	2.7	3.9
Machinery & transportation	110.4	54.8	39.5	16.1
Electrical	154.1	102.1	19.6	32.4
Other manufacturing	8.9	6.5	1.0	1.4
Other industry	52.5	32.9	9.7	9.4

Source: Statistics Canada, *Industrial R & D Expenditure in Canada,* Ottawa, 1974

Secondly, the concentration of industrial R & D in chemicals and the electrical and electronics section is evident in all countries. The defence oriented R & D expenditures of the UK and the US boost their efforts in aerospace research and development though this does not necessarily result in great overall economic benefit. The transport industry, other than aerospace, and the machinery industry are also research active in all the countries discussed except the UK. There, R & D is more heavily concentrated in fewer industries than in any other country.

Finally, the high share of government funding for industrial R & D is apparent in the US and the UK and is well above that in Japan and West Germany. However, in Japan and West Germany the government R & D effort has been more heavily oriented towards fundamental research in contrast to the United Kingdom and the United States where this area of research and development activity has not increased since 1967. Government funded R & D in the UK and US is also heavily defence oriented.

Research and development is only part of the input which results in industrial innovation, so R & D expenditure figures only convey information about part of the innovation process, and even then it needs careful interpretation. Furthermore R & D expenditures measure the cost of the R & D inputs and do not in any way measure the success of the activity. Unsuccessful research and development programmes also incur costs and are included in the expenditure data while changes in the productivity of research and development programmes are obviously ignored in the data. On the other hand, some successful innovations stem from individual inventors or from shop floor improvements and the costs involved are not included in R & D expenditure data. It follows then, that these figures are only a guide to the level and pace of industrial innovation and other evidence is required before general conclusions can be arrived at.

B. THE NUMBER OF SCIENTISTS AND ENGINEERS EMPLOYED ON R & D

Another broad indicator of industrial innovation is the number of scientists and engineers employed on R & D work. This indicator is also "rough and ready". First, it relates only to R & D. Second, it is difficult to distinguish between scientists, engineers and technicians, and thirdly, each country uses different definitions.

Figure 3
R & D Scientists/Engineers per 10,000 of the Labour Force by Country 1965-75

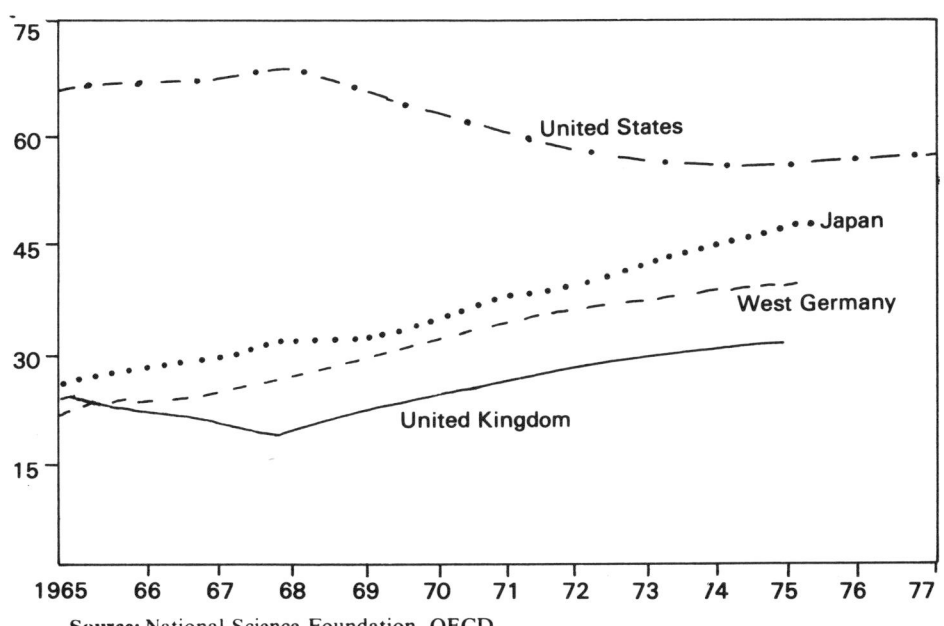

Source: National Science Foundation, OECD

Table 8
Scientists and Engineers Engaged on UK Industrial R & D
December 1975

	Thousands		
	Total	Private Industry	Other
TOTAL MANUFACTURING:....................	59.2	52.6	6.6
Chemical & allied products............	11.7	11.2	0.5
Mechanical engineering.................	4.6	3.1	1.4
Electrical engineering....................	18.0	15.9	2.0
Motor vehicles...............................	4.0	3.9	0.1
Aerospace.......................................	9.7	9.7	—
Textiles & man-made fibres............	1.3	1.1	0.2
All other manufacturing.................	9.9	7.7	2.4
NON-MANUFACTURING........................	2.5	0.6	1.8
Total..	61.7	53.2	8.4

Source: Central Statistical Office, *Economic Trends*, July 1979

Nevertheless, this indicator behaves in basically the same way as the R & D expenditure figures. The ratio of the number of R & D scientists and engineers to the total labour force is shown in Figure 3. In the United States there was a decline in the early seventies and the ratio then levelled. Japan, West Germany and the UK all increased the ratio of scientist and engineers in the labour force during the seventies.

The United Kingdom nevertheless, continues to be the worst performer in industry comparisons; the employment of personnel by industry on R & D there fell by about 40,000 over the 1967-75 period[7]. The increase in the UK ratio in Figure 3 is only because of increasing government employment of R & D personnel. Japan and West Germany do not have employment ratios higher than the US but their rate of increase is clearly higher.

The concentration in employment of these scientists and engineers in industrial sectors in the UK is similar to that of total R & D expenditure and is shown in Table 8.

---

7 Central Statistical Office, *Economic Trends*, July 1979.

Table 9
R & D Scientists and Engineers Employed in US industry
January 1978

	Thousands	Percentage
Chemical & allied products	48.3	12.1%
Machinery	58.0	14.5
Electrical & communication	85.4	21.3
Transportation (including aerospace)	109.8	27.4
Professional & scientific instruments	21.5	5.4
All other industry	77.1	19.3
TOTAL: ALL INDUSTRY	400.1	100.00

Source: National Science Foundation, *R & D in Industry*. Washington D.C. 1979

The disproportionate numbers employed in the UK chemical, electrical engineering (including electronics) and aerospace industries is again evident from the table.

The US industry disposition is shown in Table 9.

Table 10
Personnel Engaged in R & D in Industry in Canada, 1974

	Thousands	Percentage
Mines & wells	0.65	3.4%
Chemical based	4.35	22.4
Wood based	1.12	5.8
Metals	2.23	11.5
Machinery & transportation	3.42	17.6
Electrical	5.57	28.6
Other manufacturing	.33	1.7
Other industry	1.75	9.0
TOTAL INDUSTRY	19.40	100.00

Source: Statistics Canada, *Industrial R & D Expenditure in Canada*, Ottawa

Scientists and engineers engaged in research and development in the United States are concentrated in four industries: chemicals, machinery, electrical and transportation. The manufacture of professional and scientific instruments is also employing significant numbers, while it is notable that the employment of scientists and engineers doing R & D in the petroleum refining and extraction industry has been increasing since 1977. By January 1978 there were 9,900 employed and the expansion continues.

The total of all personnel employed on R & D in Canadian industry in 1974 is shown in Table 10.

The concentration of personnel engaged in R & D in Canada is in four industries: chemicals, machinery and transportation, and the electrical industry. This pattern corresponds to the R & D expenditure figures discussed previously.

Employment in R & D as an indicator of innovation is clearly limited. It is restricted to one part of the innovation process and measures one of the inputs into research and development. It contains no measure of quality, or success, or productivity but it does nevertheless confirm the trends of research and development that have already been identified and highlights one aspect of innovation activity.

C. PATENT APPLICATIONS

Another measure of innovation *output* is the application for patents. Like other indicators related to this topic, it too should be treated with caution. For instance, some patents cover major discoveries; some are almost trivial. Patent law varies in different countries and the propensity to patent also varies in different industries. The purpose of a patent can also be widely different. Some are taken out to block out competitors and some are simply filed for subsequent use. Bearing these limitations in mind, the number of patent applications filed in various countries is listed in Table 11. One fact stands out. The number of patent applications filed in Japan is consistently higher than in any other country (well over 50% higher than in the United States) and it is the only country to increase the number of patents filed over the 1970-76 period when Japanese residents filed 26% more than in 1970.

In the United States the overall number of patents filed between 1970 and 1976 did not change much largely because non-residents increased their share at the expense of residents, whose number of new registrations fell by 17%. On the basis of this indicator the United States is now importing more technical

Table 11

Patent Applications Filed 1970-76 in Selected OECD Countries

	1970	1973	1976	% change 1970-76
UNITED KINGDOM: TOTAL	62,101	60,312	54,561	-14%
OF WHICH: non resident	36,874	37,840	32,764	-12
resident	25,227	22,472	21,797	-16
CANADA: TOTAL	30,510	28,961	26,163	-16
OF WHICH: non resident	28,524	27,055	24,324	-17
resident	1,986	1,906	1,839	- 8
UNITED STATES: TOTAL	103,175	104,079	102,344	- 1
OF WHICH: non resident	26,980	37,144	37,294	+28
resident	76,195	66,935	65,050	-17
WEST GERMANY: TOTAL	66,132	66,223	61,705	- 7
OF WHICH: non resident	33,360	34,314	30,640	- 9
resident	32,772	31,909	31,065	- 5
JAPAN: TOTAL	130,829	144,814	161,016	+19
OF WHICH: non resident	30,318	29,593	25,254	- 20
resident	100,511	115,221	135,762	+26
FRANCE: TOTAL	47,283	47,234	39,890	-18
OF WHICH: non resident	33,177	33,776	28,419	-17
resident	14,106	13,458	11,471	-23

Source: *Industrial Property Statistics,* Geneva, World Intellectual Property Organisation.

know-how, particularly from Japan, West Germany and the United Kingdom[8].

The Canadian situation is different. The total number of patents filed fell by 16% between 1970 and 1976 but those of Canadian residents fell by only 8%. Canadian residents file proportionally fewer patents in their own country (7%) than residents in any other, which emphasises the importance to Canada of imported technology.

In the United Kingdom patent applications were down by 14% over the 1970-76 period and those filed by residents fell by 16%. In West Germany the number of patents filed has also fallen but by a more modest 7% over the 1970-76 period and resident patent filing in West Germany was down by only 5% in the same period.

---

[8] Office of Technology Assessment and Forecasting, *7th Report,* Department of Commerce, Washington D.C., 1977.

An analysis of the industry concentration of patents in these countries leads to similar conclusions as those derived from examining patterns of R & D expenditure referred to earlier. There is a very high correlation, ranging from 0.98 to 0.77, between industrial R & D expenditure and patent filing in particular sectors. The only industry where R & D expenditure and patent filing is not highly correlated is aerospace[9]. This is partly because of the defence orientation of much of the R & D undertaken in this sector.

To sum up: The information derived from an examination of patent applications reinforces the conclusion that innovation is concentrated in a few industries and emphasises in a dramatic way the relatively better innovative performances of Japan and West Germany. The evidence from this source also points to the decline of industrial innovation in Britain and the United States and to the growing importance of imports of technology into the United States and Canada, particularly from Japan and West Germany.

D. TECHNOLOGY TRANSFERS

In the innovation process a particular firm need not develop all, or even some, of the technology required; part or all of it can be acquired from elsewhere. This will involve royalty payments and licence fees and an examination of information about these will give some indication of the trends of technology acquired in this way. As with other indicators there are problems with the use of royalty payments as an innovation activity indicator[10]. For instance, royalty payments are often for services not connected with technology and in most records little breakdown is provided of the payment. Again, payments between firms that are affiliated are likely to be different from payments between unaffiliated and unrelated firms. Nevertheless, the data provides an indication of trends in technology transfer.

It has already been noted that Canada imports much of its technology and Table 12 lists the payments by Canadian firms for foreign technology in 1965, 1971 and 1976.

---

9 See: Pavitt, K. and Soete, L. "Innovative Activity & Export Shares" in K. Pavitt (ed.), *Technical Innovation & British Economic Performance,* Macmillan, London 1980.

10 See for instance: Taplin, M. F., US International Transactions in Royalties & Fees, *Survey of Current Business,* US Department of Commerce, December 1973.

Table 12
Payments and Receipts by Canadian Firms for Industrial Technology
(millions of Canadian dollars)

Year	Payments for foreign technology	Receipts from abroad for Canadian technology
1965	C$27.6m	C$3.0m
1971	57.6	5.5
1976	127.8	7.7

Source: *Annual Review of Science Statistics*, 1978

The net balance of payments in this table is always negative and payments by Canadians to foreigners are increasing faster than Canadian receipts. When this data is compared with direct investment flows and total royalty payments in a range of countries it seems that these technology transfer statistics tend to understate the size of the transfer of technology to Canada[11].

The net receipts in the United States for overseas royalty transactions and licensing fees are shown in Table 13. Though it has a positive balance of payments position on technology transfer the strength of this position appears to be weakening. It compares unfavourably with Japan where between 1971 and 1977 technology transfer exports expanded 3.4 times, and technology transfer imports expanded only 1.4 times. The Japanese technology transfer is

Table 13
Net US Receipt of Royalties & Licensing Fees

Year	Net Receipts (millions of US dollars)	Average % Change over previous 5 years
1967	$ 743m	+17.0%
1971	1,369	+14.2
1976	2,589	+12.4

Source: US Department of Commerce, Bureau of Economic Analysis, June 1978

---

11 See: Taplan, *op.cit.*

apparently becoming more favourable for them[12]. Complex price effects are tangled up in these figures but the general conclusions appear valid.

In the United Kingdom, net receipts from overseas technological royalty transactions have been erratic during the early seventies ranging from only £3.9 million in 1975 to £68.5 million in 1976. Manufacturing industry net receipts are also erratic ranging from minus £19.23 million in 1974 to plus £13.2 million in 1976. Typically in the seventies manufacturing firms in the UK have been a net importer of technology although the chemical industry has been an exception with positive, but declining, net receipts for technology payments.

E. SUMMARY

While it is not possible to devise a single indicator of innovation activity in industry, this chapter has analysed several general indicators. All tell much the same story. The rate of industrial innovation generally is falling in North America and Britain and resources devoted to research and development, while perhaps adequate in some industries, is generally far from sufficient to ensure that the United Kingdom, Canada and the United States remain competitive in world markets.

Industrial innovation in the United Kingdom is declining The concentration of innovation in the UK in a few industries is also more evident than in any other country. Only the chemical and electronics industries devote a relatively large share of funds to innovation; and government funding for industrial innovation is almost entirely allocated to the electronics industry and aerospace. The latter reflects the large defence orientation of the UK economy when compared to its competitors. The US is the only other country which devotes such a large share of its R & D resources to defence purposes.

In Canada the level of real resources devoted to industrial innovation appears to have remained steady since 1967 and the relative share of resources devoted to encouraging innovation has also been fairly constant. The remarkable feature of the Canadian economy is the high proportion of imported technology that contributes to innovation. Given the very close links between the Canadian and US economies, this is not surprising and Canadians

---

12 *Fuji Bank Bulletin*, November 1979.

may gain much of this technology at little direct economic cost though there may well be other less tangible costs. Their own industrial innovation is concentrated in the electrical, chemical, machinery and transportation industries. Government funds for industrial innovation are spread across industry groups more evenly than in the UK although machinery and transportation industries are the major recipients, receiving over 30% of these government funds.

In the United States the absolute level of industrial innovation is higher than anywhere else in the world but there is a marked relative decline occuring and the share of resources devoted to industrial innovation is also falling. These trends in the United States are of particular concern because of the very large contribution that country makes to world technology and innovation. The pace of increase in innovation in the United States is much slower than that of Japan and West Germany where it has increased in both real terms and in terms of the share of resources devoted to it. The concentration of innovation in the United States is in the electronics, chemical, machinery, aerospace and other transport industries. Government funding for industrial innovation is heavily concentrated in aerospace and the electronics industry; nevertheless the share of resources devoted to innovation by government appears to be falling, largely as a result of cut-backs in defence and space programmes.

In Japan the relative increase in industrial innovation has been particularly dramatic. It is also significant that the fundamental research effort in Japan and West Germany has increased while in the United Kingdom and the United States efforts in this field have remained constant and in Canada the increase has been relatively small. The indicators show that a decline in industrial innovation activity in the United Kingdom, Canada and the United States is taking place compared with other countries and that the UK is experiencing an absolute decline. There will be important consequences if these trends continue for both the total world economy and for the three countries with which this report is concerned.

II. Innovation and the Economy

The evidence of a relative decline in the resources devoted to innovation in the United Kingdom, Canada and the United States has been presented in the previous chapter. The indicators discussed are all admittedly crude but the striking feature is the similar pattern of decline they show. Industrial innovation enables either similar levels of output to be sustained using less resources, or the introduction of new and improved products or services or ways of producing or distributing. The impact of this innovation on the economy is considerable. Beside increasing profitability, it also affects productivity, investment, employment and trade.

A. INNOVATION, PRODUCTIVITY AND GROWTH

Innovation has been a crucial contributing factor to economic growth and investment by industry in innovation has frequently yielded very high rates of return. McCulloch has evaluated the economic contribution of improved technology in four ways[13]. These focus in turn on the return from individual innovations, the return from research and development in individual firms, the return from research and development in industries, and the contribution of technological change to the economy as a whole.

Studies of the rates of return on individual innovations compare the full costs of implementing these with the value of the new or improved product or process. For instance, Griliches has assessed the return on hybrid corn, Peterson on a new form of poultry breeding and Weisbrod on a polio vaccine. The estimated internal rates of return were 37% for hybrid corn, 33% for the poultry breeding technique and from 9% to 13% for polio vaccine[14]. These studies relate only to the individual innovation and no generalisation can be made from them about the rate of return on all innovation.

Attempts have been made in the United States to estimate the rate of return on research and development expenditure within individual firms. Total R & D expenditure is related to productivity growth in each firm and the rate has been assessed at between 7% and 54% over a wide range of 833 different firms[15]. The firms included those making chemical, pharmaceutical and petroleum products. The estimates of rates of return on research and development within a firm tend to understate the value of the new technology to the economy as a whole. Increased productivity in one firm will

---

13   McCulloch, R., *Research & Development as a Determinant of US International Competitiveness*, National Planning Association, Washington, 1978.
14   Ibid.
15   McCulloch, *op. cit.* p. 17.

have spill-over effects and increase the productivity in other firms in the same industry. In addition new or improved products or lower costs of production in one industry will raise productivity in other industries that purchase these new or improved or cheaper products. This will occur even if the purchasing industry does no research itself. Furthermore, these rate of return measures largely omit the benefits to consumers of new, cheaper, or improved products.

Studies of manufacturing industry in the United States have assessed the rate of return on industrial research and development in the sector as being in the range of 20%-62%[16]. However, the rate of return does depend on the source of funds for innovation. Terleckyj and Griliches estimated that the rate of return on research and development in manufacturing industry that was funded by government was zero[17]. The reason for this is that government-funded research and development in manufacturing industry is typically not directly aimed at an economic objective. It is to finance a project that is, for example, space or defence oriented and is carried out under contract for the government. Government financed research and development aimed at an economic objective is, however, more productive. For instance, between 1948-66, US government research and development directed at increasing agricultural productivity showed high returns.

The estimates of a rate of return of between 20% and 62% on industrial research and development in manufacturing also may underestimate the total benefit to the economy since such studies do not reveal the productivity gains to one industry that result from innovation in another. These cross-industry gains are impossible to quantify exactly because the sphere of impact of any innovation is difficult to measure. For example, the medical technique that delays blood clotting is now applied to Malaysian rubber trees where delayed clotting increases the latex flow. Thus the impact of an innovation in one sector may extend to other sectors in a quite different industrial classification. An attempt by Terleckyj[18] to estimate the returns on research and development expenditure in different sectors of the US economy to that in which

---

16 Freeman, R. B., Investment in Human Capital and Knowledge, in Shapiro, E. & White, W. L. (eds), *Capital for Productivity and Jobs*, Prentice Hall, New Jersey, 1977.

17 Terleckyj, N. E., *Effect of Research and Development on the Productivity Growth of Industries: An Exploratory Study*, National Planning Association, Washington, 1974 Griliches, Z., Research Expenditures & Growth Accounting, in *Science & Technology in Economic Growth*, ed. Williams, B. R., John Wiley, New York, 1973.

18 Terleckyj, N. E., *op.cit.*

it originated found these to be statistically significant and very high at around 83% for all US industry.

At the aggregate level of the economy the impact of technology has been estimated using a "residual" method. Growth in aggregate output is related to the growth of all quantifiable inputs and the residual of unexplained growth is attributed to advances in technology and other "not elsewhere classified" factors. This measure is obviously rough but if the proportion of errors included in the estimate does not shift over time it can give some indication of changes in the contribution of technology to economic growth.

Table 14

Index of Real GDP per Employee, Selected Countries

(1967 = 100)

Year	US	Canada	UK	France	W. Germany	Japan
1967	100	100	100	100	100	100
1968	102	105	103	102	105	112
1969	103	106	105	108	112	125
1970	100	108	107	114	117	135
1971	104	112	111	118	120	142
1972	108	115	115	125	126	155
1973	110	118	122	130	131	167
1974	106	117	120	133	134	168
1975	107	117	119	135	135	170
1976	110	120	122	142	145	180
1977	112	122	125	145	150	188
1978	113	122	128	148	152	195

Source: US Department of Labour, Bureau of Labour Statistics, Office of Productivity and Technology, 1979.

A recent estimate of the growth rate per employee in the US was 2.6% per year over the 1948-73 period. The contribution of advances in knowledge, and "not elsewhere classified" factors, was 1.4% or about 53% of the contribution to economic growth over that period[19]. This of course assumes a constant relation between the "not elsewhere classified" factors and advances in knowledge which is not easy to assess.

Hence, on the basis of all these different types of studies, it can be concluded that innovation has been a major contributor

---

19 Edward F. Denison, *Accounting for Slower Economic Growth: the United States in the Seventies*, Brookings Institution, Washington, 1979.

to productivity and economic growth. This implies that one of the consequences of the decline in industrial innovation may be a slowdown in productivity and there certainly is evidence of such a development.

Productivity in any economy can be measured by the change in gross domestic product per employee. Trends in productivity since 1967 are shown in Table 14 where it will be seen that the increase in labour productivity in the United States is noticeably less than in any other of the selected countries and the relatively better performances of France, West Germany and Japan stand out. In Japan over the 1967-78 period the growth in productivity is 100% compared to increases of about 50% in France and West Germany, 25% in Canada and the United Kingdom and only 13% in the United States. In the latter three countries the increases in productivity have been considerably lower since 1973.

The productivity slow-down in the United States is being treated seriously and has recently been thoroughly investigated by Denison[20]. The results are shown in Table 15. His "residual" method study focused on the productivity decline after 1973 and compared the growth in the US from 1948-73 with that between 1973-76. The most interesting and puzzling feature of his work is the changes that took place between the two periods. In particular, advances in knowledge and what he terms "other not elsewhere classified factors" seem no longer to be contributing to growth. The growth rate per employee in the latter period was negative at −0.6% with only changes in the education characteristics of the labour force, changes in investment and increasing economies of scale contributing to growth in a positive way.

This study seems to be suggesting that new knowledge no longer contributes to economic growth in the United States and this stands in stark contrast to its major contribution in the earlier 1948-73 period[21]. However, the residual method may mask another major negative factor, a matter to which we shall return.

Another US study by Z. Griliches also supports Denison's findings[22]. Professor Griliches uses a different method for estimating the contribution of research and development expenditures to economic growth in the manufacturing industry. He notes an uneven decline in productivity in manufacturing industry in the

---

20 Edward F. Denison, *op.cit.*
21 The analysis used in the Denison study attributes everything not classified into this residual factor of "advances in knowledge". It is in this sense a measure of ignorance.
22 Griliches, Z., *Research and Development and the Productivity Slowdown*, mimeo, 1979. Paper presented at the American Economic Association Meetings, Atlanta, Georgia. December 28, 1979.

Table 15
Sources of Growth of National Income per Employee, in the Non-residential Business Sector of the United States, 1948-73 and 1973-76

	1948-73	1973-76
Adjusted growth rate per employee per year	2.6%	−0.6%
Changes in labour characteristics:		
Hours at work	−0.2	−0.5
Age-sex composition	−0.5	0.3
Education	0.5	0.9
Changes in capital and land per employee:		
Non-residential structures and equipment	0.3	0.2
Inventories	0.1	0
Land	0	0
Improved allocation of resources	.4	0
Legal and human environment	0	−0.4
Economies of scale from larger markets	.4	0.2
Advances in knowledge and "not elsewhere classified" factors	1.4	−0.7

Source: Edward F. Denison, *op.cit.* footnote 17.

US during the seventies and concludes that for the 1959-68 period, research and development contributed at least one-tenth of manufacturing economic growth. But in the 1969-77 period the contribution of research and development to manufacturing productivity appears to have fallen to zero. Both reduced research and development expenditures and a collapse in the productivity of research and development itself, in manufacturing, leads to the *prima facie* conclusion that it no longer contributes to manufacturing growth in the United States.

These US studies have not been repeated using Canadian or UK data so it is not yet known whether the apparent contribution of R & D in these economies has also collapsed. However, the relatively slow productivity increases in both Canada and the United Kingdom imply that at least some of the problems expressed in the US may also be at work in these economies. For this reason it is worth asking why recent technology appears to be so dramatically less productive than it has been in previous periods.

One explanation takes the data at face value and argues that innovation has actually become unproductive. A large fraction of innovation activity has been diverted away from the type of innovation that adds to measured productivity and directed towards innovation needed to comply with various environmental and regulatory constraints. The latter type of innovation may have some social benefit but the benefit does not show up in productivity measures. But not all industries have been subject to the same regulatory pressures and the overall impact of regulation on measured productivity may, therefore, be quite small. Denison has estimated the regulatory contribution to growth at $-.22\%$ per year[23]. This negative effect from regulation is larger than in the sixties but is not that great.

Nevertheless some industries, notably pharmaceuticals and pesticides, have been more affected by regulation than others. The cost of introducing an average major pharmaceutical innovation in the OECD area has risen from $1.2 million in 1962 to about $54 million in 1976 and much of this cost increase has occurred because of the increased time spent on testing and approval. Partly as a result of this, the number of new chemical entities marketed in the US and Europeean countries has fallen by about 50% between 1960 and 1973[24]. Whether or not the social benefits of the regulation outweigh the costs, needs more consideration. Massive deregulation could increase social costs dramatically and turn out to be socially disastrous. This is essentially a political issue.

Another reason for a decline in the overall productivity of innovation is the new emphasis being made on innovation that is more short term and non-risky. In the United States more industrial research and development is being diverted towards the improvement of existing products and away from the development of new products and processes. A recent survey by McGraw Hill found that in 1976, 58% of industrial research and development was aimed at the improvement of products compared to about 45% in the earlier seventies. At the same time the percentage of total sales expected from new products had fallen from 16% in the early seventies to 13% in 1978[25]. This trend towards "improvement" innovation in the OECD area was also confirmed by a study of innovation in the electronics, machine-tools, pharmaceuticals, fertilizer and pesticide industries, published in 1979[26].

There is, therefore, evidence to suggest that as well as a relative decline in innovation there is also a trend towards those

---

23 Edward F. Denison, *op.cit.*
24 OECD. *Science and Technology in the New Socio-Economic Context*, Paris, 1979.
25 *Business Plans for Research and Development Expenditures*, McGraw Hill, New York.
26 OECD, *op.cit.*

innovations which yield less return and are either less risky or directed towards meeting regulatory requirements.

But this is not the whole explanation for the apparent collapse in innovative productivity. Innovation may be still productive but its contribution to growth and productivity is not being measured by the method used in recent studies of Griliches and Denison. Both studies implicitly assume that firms are operating on the boundary of their technical production constraints. This seems unlikely in the current climate of uncertainty about future absolute and relative prices and the resulting fluctuations in capacity utilization. As a result the contribution of innovation is not being properly measured in these studies and the uncertainty prevailing in the current economic climate is causing behaviour which is swamping out the measured contribution of technological change.

Thus, there is evidence to suggest that the productivity slowdown is being caused in part by declining innovation and in part by a trend towards innovations yielding lower but more certain returns. At the same time, the productivity slowdown itself and the current economic climate are reinforcing the decline in innovation, which in turn has important implications for price behaviour. There is not a straightforward relationship between prices and productivity but there is evidence to suggest that more productive industries exhibit a tendency to both lower prices and higher wages. A simple regression across all US industries suggests that a 1% increase in real productivity per person-hour leads to a relative price decrease of 76% and a small increase in real wages in the industry concerned[27]. Fighting inflation thus demands productivity increases and it is notable that those industries which are innovation intensive are also more productive. For instance, the electronics and chemical industries in the UK, Canada and the US are all research intensive, productive and over the 1974-77 period, show relative price decreases for their products. Increasing innovation not only increases productivity in the innovative sector but keeps prices in that sector rising less rapidly than the general price level.

B. INNOVATION, INVESTMENT AND EMPLOYMENT

The decision to innovate is intimately connected at the company level with investment and employment decisions and these in turn feed back and affect growth and productivity. The positive relationship between investment and productivity is shown in

---

27 Henrik S. Houthakker, Growth and Inflation: Analysis by Industry, *Brookings Papers on Economic Activity*, Vol. I, 1979.

Figure 4 where Japan, France and West Germany all display high productivity increases accompanied by a high proportion of national resources devoted to investment. On the other hand the US, Canada and the UK have devoted less resources to investment and achieved markedly lower productivity increases in manufacturing.

This poor growth performance in the UK, Canada and the US has also led to higher rates of unemployment in these countries

Figure 4
Investment and Productivity, Selected Countries 1960-76

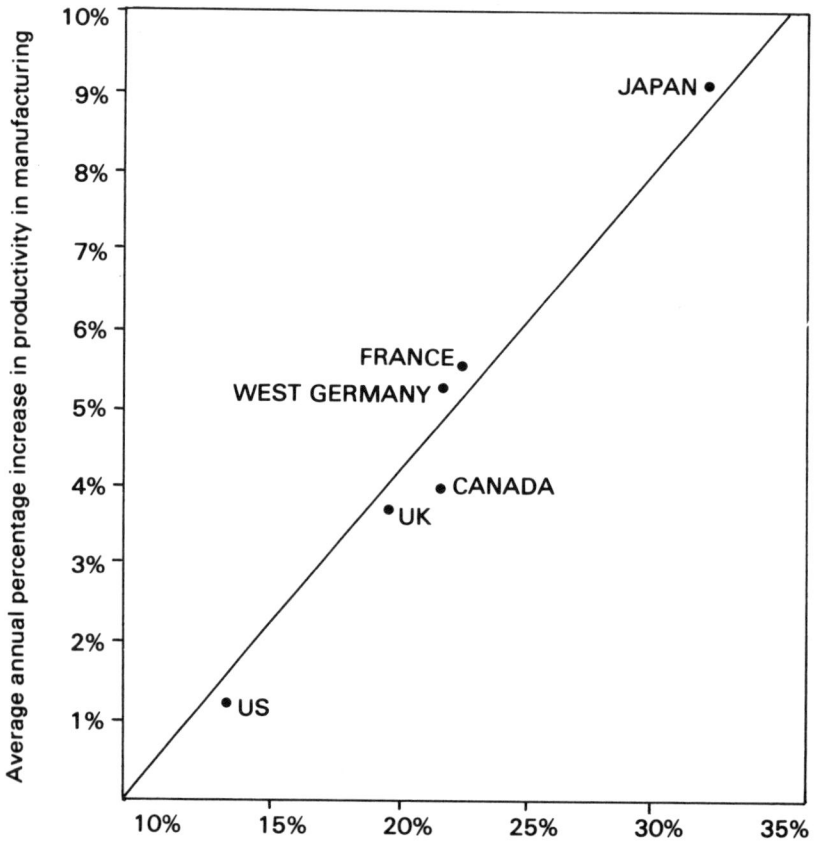

Average annual ratio of non-residential fixed investment to GNP

Source: American Productivity Center Inc., *Productivity Perspectives*, and Bureau of Labour Statistics, US Department of Labour.

Table 16
Percentage of Labour Force Unemployed 1974-1978

	1974	1976	1978
United Kingdom	2.5%	5.4%	5.7%
Canada	5.4	7.2	8.4
United States	5.6	7.7	6.0
France	2.3	4.2	4.8
West Germany	2.7	4.7	4.3
Japan	1.4	2.0	2.2

Source: OECD, *Economic Outlook* and *Selected Economic Indicators*.

as Table 16 shows. While all countries have registered some increase in the rates of unemployment, the relatively high economic growth rates in West Germany and Japan have enabled them to maintain relatively higher employment levels.

Innovation necessarily entails new investment and the relative decline in innovation in the United Kingdom, Canada and the United States has also been accompanies by a relative decline in the resources devoted to investment. Over the 1960-77 period only 9.1% of US output (at factor cost), was devoted to capital investment; in the UK and Canada the proportion was 13.5% and 14.7%. In Japan 28.8% of output was devoted to investment during 1960-74 and in West Germany about 16% of total resources went to investment[28].

The pattern of investment also appears to have shifted in all countries. For instance, a lesser share of total industrial investment is generally devoted to non-residential construction, indicating a slowdown in the development of new capacity. Recent investment is mainly directed to installing equipment and machinery which is replacing and modernising existing plant but this does not necessarily add significantly to potential output. In Canada the share of non-residential construction in all investment has fallen from 62% to 50% over the 1960-75 period; in the United States the fall has been from 44% to 32% and in the United Kingdom non-residential construction has remained fairly steady at 35% of all investment. In Japan non-residential construction as a share of total investment has fallen from 65% to 48% over the 1960-75 period and in West Germany the decline has been less rapid, falling from 48% in 1960 to 40% in 1975[29].

---

[28] Calculated from figures of US Department of Labour, Bureau of Labour Statistics.
[29] Annex to *Towards Full Employment & Price Stability*, OECD Paris, 1977.

Figure 5

Summary of the Quantitative and Qualitative Impacts of Technical Change on Employment in a Number of Industries

	Agriculture	Coal mining	Canadian Railways	Textile Machinery	Textile Industry	Cement Industry	Steel Industry	Metalworking Industry	NC machine tools	Computer-aided design	Automation
Reduction in labour force	✓	✓			✓						
Increased output with same or reduced labour force (jobless growth)	✓	✓	✓		✓		✓	✓	✓	✓	✓
De-skilling or making certain skills redundant	✓		✓	✓	✓	✓				✓	✓
Generated the need for new skills	✓	✓	✓	✓	✓	✓	✓		✓	✓	✓
Reduction in job satisfaction				✓	✓	✓		✓	✓		✓
Required higher level management skills	✓				✓	✓				✓	✓
Displacement of specialist skills outside the factory				✓	✓						
Job loss due to lack of technical change competitiveness							✓		✓		

Source: R. Rothwell and W. Zeyveld, *Technical Change & Employment*, Francis Pinter, London 1979

This behaviour of investment indicators is in line with the trend in innovative activity towards more short term and less risky projects. Expectations about the future are so confused that few firms are planning major capacity expansion.

Within manufacturing industry investment is concentrated in those sectors that also tend to be more innovative. Chemicals and electrical (including electronics) accounted for 16% to 23% of all manufacturing investment in the UK, Canada and the US with the other predominant investment sector being the petroleum and natural gas industries in each country.

The impact of technical change upon employment has been studied in several industries in the UK, Canada and the US and the results are summarised in Figure 5. In most industries innovation led to the ability to produce similar levels of output with less people employed. This did not necessarily lead to a reduction in the labour force in the innovating industry since in many cases output expanded and this absorbed the technologically displaced workers. It is notable that in most industries the innovation itself generated a need for new skills amongst the work force and required higher levels of skill amongst management. In the process certain skills became redundant but overall, innovation makes qualitative impacts upon the labour force as well as quantitative ones.

On the quantative side it is frequently feared that innovation will cause more unemployment, through its labour-saving bias, than the additional employment it will generate through its tendency to increase output. A major study of this problem by the US National Commission on Technology in 1966 came to the conclusion that if unemployment occurred due to innovation then expansionary economic policies would quickly generate new jobs in sufficient numbers to offset any labour displacement involved in the introduction of new technology[30].

The economic growth in the United States during the 1950's and 1960's certainly supported this conclusion. The proportion of the workforce employed in manufacturing fell steadily as manufacturing output increased and the share of people employed in service industries grew. Technical advance in service industries was less rapid and the increasing demand and supply of both services and manufactured goods enabled full employment to be maintained. This pattern of behaviour held in all developed and industrialised countries.

---

30 *National Commission on Technology, Automation & Economic Progress, Technology & the American Economy,* Washington D.C., 1966.

Recently a more gloomy outlook has been suggested by Freeman and other European commentators compared to that of their North American colleagues[31]. They emphasise the structural shift in employment away from manufacturing towards services and proceed to analyse the implications of this. The first point they make is that unemployment is relatively high in most developed countries, but there is little sign that these high levels of unemployment are inducing a fall in wage costs. This in turn means that labour saving innovations will continue in an attempt to lower industrial costs. Further, they suggest that the current wave of innovations is expected to make a major impact on the service sector as well as on manufacturing. In particular labor-saving microelectronic innovations streamline office procedures causing some clerks and typists to be replaced by systems that collect, store, transmit and manipulate information. Thus labour-saving innovations are now expected to occur in services as well as in manufacturing.

Previous historical experience suggests that this technological displacement of labour is no cause for concern as long as it is accompanied by increases in real economic growth. Unfortunately in the early 1980's there is little likelihood of more than a small increase in output as investment is not being aimed at capacity expansion. In any case this school of economists argue that the increase in output that is needed, now and in the future, to absorb the surplus labour is massive. For these reasons the effects of new innovations on employment may be negative.

The view taken on the employment effect largely depends upon the degree of optimism held about the chances of output increasing. The chances for production increases of the required size seem more likely in Japan and West Germany than in the UK, Canada and the US. But all countries are influenced by the total international economic climate and the absolute size of the United States means that its recovery is critical for all nations if the structural changes taking place are to lead to improved efficiency and increasing employment.

It is worth noting that the decline in employment in manufacturing industry has been less in those sectors which have previously been identified as innovation intensive. In the UK between 1973 and 1977, the change in employment in the chemical industry was −0.1%, the lowest decline of any broad manufacturing category. In the US employment in chemicals over this period

---

31 Freeman, C., *Technical Change and Employment*, Six Countries Programme on Aspects of Government Policies towards Technological Innovation in Industry, mimeo, 1978.

actually increased by 0.5% while total manufacturing employment declined by −0.8%. Any moves towards Luddite policies must be avoided; employment is more comparatively enhanced by increasing innovation than by decreasing it. A decline in innovation simply implies a falling capability to compete and eventually lowers production and employment. This point becomes clearer when the effect of innovation on trade is considered.

C. INNOVATION AND TRADE

Innovation is a major factor in explaining changes in the patterns of international trade. Its effects, however, vary between industries. Posner has suggested that a product innovation is exported at least until imitators come into the market and if the "imitation lag" is longer than the "demand lag" then technology-gap trade persists[32]. Several factors help to maintain this technology gap for fairly long periods; they include the quality and scale of research and development, the "clustering" of innovations and dynamic economies of scale. Once a new product technology matures, traditional factor-cost elements become increasingly important in explaining reasons for trade. An empirical study of trade in synthetic materials[33] and studies reviewing the electronic components and the chemical industry confirm this[34].

This theory is clearly relevant for those industries which introduce new products, such as the capital goods and chemical industries, but its applicability is less obvious in consumer goods industries and in the production of basic materials. In capital goods and chemicals there is typically much research and development and it is directed mainly at the design and development of product innovations.

In basic materials industries the output generally tends to be standardised and innovation occurs largely through the introduction of new capital intensive processes which are directed to cost saving and may be reproduced elsewhere. In consumer good industries fashion-based design and advertising are often

---

32 Posner, M. V., International Trade and Technical Change, *Oxford Economic Papers*, October 1961.

33 Hufbauer, G., *Synthetic Materials in International Trade* Harvard University Press, Cambridge, Mass., 1966.

34 Golding A. M., *The semi-conductor industry in Britain and the US*, D. Phil. thesis, Sussex University, 1972.

  Scriberras, E., *Multinational Electronic Companies and National Economic Policies*, JAI Press, New York, 1977.

Table 17
Share in the Value of Exports of Manufactures* 1950-1979

	1950	1960	1965	1970	1975	1979
United Kingdom	25.5%	16.5%	13.9%	10.8%	9.3%	9.7%
United States	27.3	21.6	20.3	18.5	17.7	15.9
France	9.9	9.6	8.8	8.7	10.2	10.5
West Germany	7.3	19.3	19.1	19.8	20.3	20.7
Japan	3.4	6.9	9.4	11.7	13.6	13.6
Italy	26.6†	5.1	6.7	7.2	7.5	8.3
Others		21.0	21.8	23.3	21.4	21.3
Total	100	100	100	100	100	100

Source: National Institute Economic Review, Statistical Appendix, Table 2.2, London. Various Issues.
* Arms excluded except in 1950. † Benelux countries, Canada, Switzerland, Sweden.

more important than innovations in producing new products. While innovations in the production process can lower costs, a more significant factor is innovation originating in the capital goods industry. Hence the record shows that R & D activity in the consumption goods sector is usually at very low levels[35].

These observations suggest that export performance in the capital goods industry and chemicals should be closely related to relative innovative performance and this turns out to be the case. Empirical work has related both R & D and patent data to export performance in these industries in the OECD countries, and found strong positive relationships[36].

It is also likely to be the case that those countries with a relatively good innovative performance will also have relatively good trade positions in basic materials and consumption goods trade. This will occur through the introduction of cost saving process innovations and enable these countries to compete in comparative cost advantage terms. Given the relative decline in innovation performance in the United Kingdom, the United States and Canada, this suggests, other things being equal, that their share in world trade will also have fallen and this is indeed what is happening in the period 1950-79 (Table 17). The US and UK's share in trade in manufactures has declined steadily since 1950. The performance of Canada is subsumed in the "other countries" category in Table 17 but its share has also declined over this period. ("Others" include Canada, Sweden, Switzerland and the Benelux countries.) It is also relevant to this discussion to note that both Japan and West Germany have increased their share of trade in manufactured goods dramatically over the period.

Of course innovation is not the only determinant of trade performance—changes in cost are another but they do not account for alteration in the patterns. For instance, in the UK, Canada and the US, unit labour costs have increased less rapidly than in other countries, as shown in Table 18, where their share of total costs in manufacturing for several countries over the 1950-77 period is compared.

---

35 Freeman, C., Technical Innovation and British Trade Performance, in Frank Blackaby (ed), *De-Industrialisation,* Heinemann, London, 1979.
36 Keith Pavitt & Luc Soete, Innovative Activities and Export Shares, in Keith Pavitt (ed), *Technical Innovation and British Economic Performance,* Macmillan London 1980.
Keesing, B, The impact of R & D on US trade *Journal of Political Economy,* February 1967.
Vernon, R., (ed), *The Technology Factor in International Trade,* NEBER, New York, 1970

Table 18
Unit Labour Costs in Manufacturing, 1950-1977
(indices based on US dollar data: 1967 = 100)

Period	UK	Canada	US	France	W. Germany	Japan
1950-54	64	91	77	87	65	87
1955-59	81	103	90	89	70	87
1960-64	91	96	96	90	88	90
1965-69	96	98	100	99	99	103
1970	106	112	117	97	126	113
1971	118	116	118	103	143	131
1972	127	122	118	118	164	160
1973	133	127	123	146	212	195
1974	160	148	143	157	236	237
1975	200	167	152	203	270	285
1976	185	187	158	191	258	285
1977	200	184	168	202	293	327

Source: US Bureau of Labour Statistics.

During the 1960-77 period unit labour costs in US manufacturing rose at an average annual rate of 3.3% while those in Japan and Germany rose at rates of 8.4% and 8.2% respectively. These disparities in Table 18 suggest that the share of world trade ought to be moving in favour of the United States, the United Kingdom and Canada but this is clearly not the case (see Table 17).

Changes in absolute (as opposed to unit) labour costs do not explain the trade share differences either, as Table 19 shows. West Germany has now overtaken the US as the highest wage earner in manufacturing and UK labour receives lower compensation than labour in any other country in the table.

Cost disadvantages of other factors of production such as capital, raw materials or energy, if they exist, are not likely to be large enough to explain the poor trade performances of these countries.

Attempts have been made by Kravis and Lipsey, using a questionnaire method, to assess the importance of all factors in trade[37]. Their study of US—W. German trade attributed the relative

---

[37] Kravis, I. & Lipsey, R. E., *Price Competitiveness in World Trade,* Columbia University Press, New York, 1971.

Table 19
Hourly Compensation of Production Workers in Manufacturing
(US dollars)

1960-77	1960	1970	1977
United Kingdom	$0.82	$1.46	$3.29
Canada	2.13	3.46	7.27
United States	2.66	4.20	7.34
West Germany	0.83	2.32	7.60
France	0.83	1.74	4.85
Japan	0.26	0.99	3.70

Source: US *International Economic Report of the President,* 1977, and updated using US Bureau of Labour Statistics.

importance of different factors to the success to US exporters in the following way:

Lower prices 28%
Product superiority 37%
After sales service 12%
Product uniqueness 10%

Relative advantages in innovation are likely to contribute favourably to each of these categories of success in export performance.

It is also notable that developing countries are increasing their share of world trade in manufactures. This is largely occurring in basic materials industries and those producing consumption goods where cost factors tend to dominate international competitiveness. The share of developing countries in the imports of industrialized nations rose from 5.7% in 1960 to 9.5% in 1976 and the World Bank forecasts that this trend will accelerate throughout the 1980's[38]. This behaviour adds to the competitive pressure that the UK, Canada and the US face and makes the relative decline in innovative activity in these nations of even greater concern[39].

---

38 *World Development Report,* The World Bank, Washington D.C., 1979
39 For an assessment of the impact that the Newly Industrialising Countries are likely to have on the economies of developed countries see N. McMullen, Newly Industrializing Countries in the World Economy, BNAC; London, Washington and Montreal (forthcoming).

D. SUMMARY

In this chapter the influence of innovation on the economy has been discussed. One major effect is its contribution to productivity and economic growth which some studies suggest may be around 30% to 50% of the growth in productivity. There is certainly sufficient evidence to conclude that those industries which are relatively more active at innovation tend to be more productive.

Productivity improvements also appear to have a positive impact in the fight against inflation. In the more productive industries, prices tend to increase less rapidly than the average inflation rate and in some productive industries, prices have declined absolutely. In addition, workers in these more productive sectors have received real wage increases as productivity increased.

In the light of this, the relative decline in innovation in the United Kingdom, Canada and the United States must be of concern. Productivity increases in these countries have only been modest and the scope to both lower prices and raise real wages has been exceedingly limited.

Low productivity increases and relatively little innovation activity also affects international trade patterns. The reduced share of world trade in manufactures that the UK, Canada and the US are experiencing seems to be in part caused by the relative decline in resources devoted to innovation. This not only affects the technical design of traded products and their relative costs, but also their quality. Thus the relative lack of innovation tends to lower international trade competitiveness which in turn adds to the economic problems already apparent in the three countries.

The relative decline in innovation has, not surprisingly, been accompanied by relatively low investment activity. Innovation usually entails some investment and they can be considered as complementary activities. The investment that has occurred has been concentrated on plant and equipment to improve processes and reduce costs of products rather than on extending capacity. This in turn implies no foreseeable large increases in output nor any large increase in employment. Innovation affects job prospects in two main ways: firstly, when innovation is capital intensive it tends to displace workers but secondly, increased production, encouraged by the innovation, can result in increased employment. This latter effect has dominated in the past but some commentators suggest that it will not do so in the future. This is of particular concern in the United Kingdom, Canada and the United States, where the capacity to compete seems to be falling and unemployment is severe.

This is not to suggest that innovation should be halted because of the possibly deleterious effects on employment. On the contrary, if innovation does not proceed the effects on employment will be even more disastrous as the three countries will become less productive and even less capable of competing in world trade. In addition the possibility of price decreases and rising living standards becomes more remote with low productivity rates and relatively declining innovation. The impact of innovation on the economy is clearly important but so too is the influence of the economy on innovation. To this we now turn.

III. The Economy and Innovation

While it has been shown that innovation has a major impact on the economy it is itself largely determined by the prevailing economic climate. This leads to the existence of a vicious circle where declining innovative activity contributes to a relatively poor economic performance and this in turn leads to a further decline in innovative activity.

A. THE ECONOMIC CLIMATE

A number of important changes occurred in the economic climate during the seventies and awareness of them was heightened by the quadrupling of oil prices at the end of 1973, though a number of changes were happening well before the "OPEC crisis". The Science Policy Research Unit at Sussex University and Staffgroup Strategic Surveys in the Netherlands have noted eight significant developments[40].

1. An increase in the inflation rate associated with steep rises in food and primary commodity prices.
2. A shift from an "adjustable peg" system of international monetary management to a "managed float" system, by countries and blocs, following the breakdown in the international exchange rate system between 1970 and 1973.
3. Rapid increases in money supply linked with an expansion of international reserves between 1970 and 1973.
4. A fall in the share of non-residential construction in total investment since the mid sixties. As mentioned earlier, this indicates a shift from capacity expansion through the construction of new factories to "rationalisation" investment based on the replacement of machinery and equipment in existing plants.
5. The concentration of industry increased and the number of small firms fell as did their share in output throughout the sixties and seventies.
6. Profit rates fell in many industrialised countries from the late 1960's.
7. Capital per person employed increased continually but capital productivity did not rise as fast and in some countries, notably the UK, Canada and the US, productivity fell.
8. Company indebtedness increased during the sixties but this rise has levelled out since the 1974-75 recession.

---

[40] *The Current International Economic Climate and Policies for Technical Innovation,* Report prepared for the Six Countries Programme on Government Policies towards Technological Innovation in Industry. November, 1977.

These changes in the economic climate in which firms operate have an important influence on their decisions about innovation. The factors which determine the level of innovation within private industry have received considerable attention from economists.

B. THE DETERMINANTS OF INNOVATION

(i) Economic Determinants

The principal economic reason for innovating in private industry is to increase profits. This occurs either through reducing costs or by increasing revenues or both. Process innovations, if successful, permit similar levels of output to be produced using less inputs and consequently costs per unit of output fall. Prices of output may then also fall, thus stimulating sales. Successful product innovations introduce new products or improvements to existing ones which will either increase or maintain sales revenue in existing markets or open up possibilities in new ones.

Hence industrial innovation is not an exogenous happening; it is determined by firms' expectations about future profits. Studies by Schmookler in 1962 and Mansfield in 1968 confirm this description of firms' behaviour[41]. Some interesting implications may be deduced from it.

The foundation for much successful innovation is an adequate technology base. This is formed from fundamental discoveries which in turn stem from access to basic research which may have occurred much earlier. Now basic research is by definition that which has no certain outcome; it is not aimed at any particular commercial application so it does not tend to make any immediate contribution to a firm or an industry's profits. As a result, industry as such performs little basic research itself and in the current economic climate in the United Kingdom, Canada and the United States the amount of basic research funded by industry has even declined relative to that of other countries.

Returns to industry on basic research are low because the knowledge acquired can only be appropriated to a limited extent. The results of such research tend to be freely available and the benefit to the total economy far outweighs the benefit to the individual firm. Because of this externality, Nelson and Arrow have argued that it is vital for government to fund a major part

---

41 Schmookler J., Economic Sources of Inventive Activity, *Journal of Economic History,* March, 1962.
Mansfield, E., *Industrial Research & Technological Innovation* Longman's, Green & Co., London, 1968.

of basic research[42]. If funding is left to individual firms the level of basic research performed will be less than socially optimal for the whole economy. The returns on basic research to an individual firm which funds it are extremely uncertain and in the current climate it is not surprising that this part of a firm's activity has been reduced.

Applied research and development is that which is aimed at a commercial application and since private firms are profit seeking they tend to favour R & D projects that are less risky, *ceteris paribus*. If the expected profit from two alternative projects is the same, but one project is more risky than another, then the low risk project is favoured. The degree of technical risk associated with applied research and development projects has been assessed in both the United States and the United Kingdom. The probability of technical success in the US on an aggregate of applied research and development projects was 0.8 and in the UK it was 0.91[43].

Technical risks in the applied research and development stage are only a small part of the uncertainty attached to innovation. Booz, Allan & Hamilton Inc. found that out of every ten projects from research and development, five failed in product and market tests and only two went on to become commercially successful[44]. This puts the chances of success at a low 0.2 and this implies that high expected returns would be needed to justify the risk of proceeding with innovation. This uncertainty aspect cannot be overstressed in the current climate. In assessing expected profitability from an innovation, estimates are made of expected sales, prices, and factor costs. These estimates hinge not only on the behaviour of the economy and the international market, but also on the behaviour of competitors. With future absolute and relative prices so uncertain, both domestically and abroad, and with demand so difficult to assess, uncertainty at present is considerably larger than the risk rates prevailing in the fifties and sixties. This high level of unpredictability coupled with falling profit expectations and return on capital is a major contributor to the decline in innovation in the industrial sector.

---

42 Nelson, R. R., The Simple Economies of Basic Scientific Research, *Journal of Political Economy*, June, 1959.
    Arrow, K. H., Economic Welfare and the Allocation of Resources for Invention, in Nelson, R. R. (ed), *The Rate and Direction of Inventive Activity*, NBER, New York, 1962.
43 Mansfield, E., The Diffusion of Eight Major Industrial Innovations in the United States in *The State of Science & Research*, West View Press, Corado, 1977 N. Terleckyj.
    Schott, Kerry. Investment in Private Industrial Research & Development in Britain, *Journal of Industrial Economics*, December 1976.
44 Booz, Allen & Hamilton Inc., *Management of New Products*, New York, 1960.

Because investment and innovation are complementary it follows that the cost of new investment has a significant bearing on the level of innovation; high capital costs obviously impede the introduction of new processes and products. Schmookler's seminal study showed that increased investment was associated with increased patent activity and when investment declined so did patenting[45]. His study covered US railroads for the 1860-1950 period but its results also apply to aggregate industrial behaviour in the last two decades[46].

A relatively low capital costs regime stimulates both investment and innovation. The components of these costs are the prices of investment goods, the costs of borrowing to finance investment and depreciation costs. Where there are high taxes, it follows that less finance is available for new investment. Similarly, innovation costs are raised when the corporate investment allowance for tax purposes and the rate at which R & D expenditure can be written off is decreased.

All these factors have important effects on research and development expenditures but they are difficult to estimate. An attempt using British industrial data looked at six theoretical policy changes that would effect R & D expenditure[47]. These were:

(i) a 1% decrease in the interest rate
(ii) a doubling of patent life
(iii) an increase in patent life from 16 to 20 years
(iv) a corporate tax decrease of 10%
(v) a corporate investment allowance increase of 10%
(vi) an increase in research and development allowance of 10%

Each of the postulated policy changes was examined within a simulation model of British private industry, and all other exogenous variables except the one to be changed were kept constant for the simulation period. The impact of a particular policy initiative was measured by the differences between what happened in the system with and without the policy change.

The essential finding was that corporate tax reductions were likely to stimulate industrial R & D more than any other policy. Patent life extension has little effect. A decrease in the interest rate and an increase in R & D allowances both stimulated R & D slightly and an increase in corporate investment allowances also

---

45 Schmookler, *op.cit.*
46 Bureau of Economic Analysis, US Department of Commerce.
47 Schott, Kerry, the Relation Between Industrial Research and Development and Factor Demands, *Economic Journal,* March 1978.

stimulated R & D and investment. However, corporate tax decreases seemed to produce by far the most effect.

A recent theoretical paper in the US also supports the general conclusions of this UK work[48]. So far no empirical work of this nature has been done using data from other countries but the high element of capital costs in innovation does intuitively suggest that a decrease in these costs would be beneficial for innovation and the UK empirical results above look sensible. In the current climate of low profitability and high interest rates, the decline in both investment and innovation is an understandable and rational response.

This discussion has so far focussed on expected returns and costs from innovation. The decision about whether to innovate or not is essentially a management decision and the quality, attitudes and interests of management are thus additional important determinants of innovation. They are particularly critical in the commercialization phase of any project where success or failure is most often determined. It may also be critical in the attention and resources provided for R & D activity. What then do we know about management attitudes?

A recent international comparison summarizes the major differences in the background and education of management in various countries[49]. Those from the United Kingdom and the United States have much in common and differ considerably from those of continental Europe. However there is a higher proportion of the US population at college and a higher proportion of college educated personnel in management.

The major differences in the background of managers are summarized in Table 20. UK managers are not as "professionalised" and the role of engineering in management is different. Less than 25% of UK managers have attended university full time. In Germany, France, Japan and the Soviet Union the importance of technical expertise is accepted and engineers are the preferred management group. In addition, in the United Kingdom industrial managers are drawn from lower social classes than in other countries. This in itself is not cause for any concern unless it reflects managerial quality differences. Finance and insurance industries and the civil service in Britain attract entrants from a higher social background

---

48 Richard E. Slitor, *Tax Incentives for Industrial Innovation Research,* Paper presented at Seven Springs Conference on Industrial Innovation. Carnegie-Mellon University, Pittsburgh, April, 1979.

49 Swords-Isherwood, Nuala, "British Management Compared" in Pavitt, K. (ed) *Technical Innovation and British Economic Performance,* Macmillan, London, 1980.

Table 20
The Different Background of Management in Selected Countries

	Great Britain	USA	W. Germany	France	USSR
Social class of managers	mixed/low	mixed/high	high/mixed	high	high
% of graduates in management	low	high	high	high	high
% of graduates in population	low	high	low	low	medium
Subjects of study and their prestige order	Liberal arts Science Engineering	Liberal arts Engineering Science	Engineering Business economics Law	Engineering	Engineering
Full-time versus Part-time education	P-T high F-T low	P-T low F-T high	P-T low F-T high	P-T low F-T high	P-T low F-T high
Likelihood of having been promoted from the shop floor	high	medium	low	low	low

Source: Swords-Isherwood, *op.cit.* Footnote[49].

than does manufacturing industry. There are cultural reasons for these differences between countries but taken together the differences in management seem to suggest that at least part of the relatively poor performance of Britain lies in the quality of its managers. Furthermore, the problem in Britain does not simply seem to be about the low supply of engineering graduates; there is little demand for them as well, and this may be caused by the existing attitudes in current British management and society. The importance of the technical expertise such graduates provide is perhaps not sufficiently recognized. These comments do not apply uniformly to all of British industry and the chemical industry is one sector that is exceptional. It is also worth pointing out that this study of managerial characteristics has ignored the social environment in which managers operate. In the United Kingdom poor industrial relations may lead to less time being available for the primary task of management and this climate could well contribute to the difficulties experienced in the United Kingdom.

These determinants of innovation have been discussed in the context of the decision to perform R & D and whether or not to proceed with commercialisation. However, diffusion of innovation throughout the economy is what really affects aggregate economic performance. There is some evidence to suggest that the pace of diffusion of process innovations in the United Kingdom is relatively slow but no country tends to lead any other in the initial introduction of new techniques[50]. Five factors seem to govern the diffusion rate. *First* the economic advantage of the innovation over existing techniques. *Second* the degree of uncertainty associated with the innovation. *Third* the extent of the commitment required, particularly in investment requirements, to implement the innovation. *Fourth* the rate of reduction of uncertainty as the innovation proceeds. *Fifth* the quality of management.

These factors have been investigated by Nabseth and Ray, and by Mansfield, and their results confirm the importance of these factors[51]. Earlier studies also support this evidence[52]. It is notable that being first with an innovation is not always an advantage and whether pioneering succeeds or not seems to be often a matter of timing. A rushed introduction means that proper tests are not

---

50 Nabseth, L & Ray, G. F., *The Diffusion of New Industrial Processes*, Cambridge University Press, Cambridge, 1974.
51 Nabseth & Ray, ibid.
  Mandfield, E., *Industrial Research and Innovation*, Longmans Green & Co., London, 1968.
52 Griliches, Z., Hybrid Corn and the Economies of Innovation, *Science*, 29th July, 1960.
  David P., The Mechanisation of Reaping in the Ante-Bellum Midwest in H. Rosovsky (ed), *Industrialisation in Two Systems*, Wiley, New York, 1966.

necessarily made before launching and failure can result. On the other hand if a competitor is first in the market, not only will existing sales fall, but sales opportunities for a competing firm can decline dramatically[53].

Innovation is thus basically determined by expected profitability and the ability of managers to see and seize the opportunities for making these profits. These factors are important in every phase of the innovation process. The current economic climate in the early 1980s is clearly affecting innovative activity in all countries but the relatively worse economic problems of the United States and Canada, and particularly the United Kingdom, are exacerbating the situation. There is also evidence to suggest that British management is not as technically equipped as management in other countries to deal with either the development or the introduction of innovations.

(ii) Institutional Factors

Dynamic and fierce competition between large firms is thought, by Schumpeterian economists, to be the major driving force influencing innovation. Large firms also compete in terms of price and quality of products and this in turn influences profit and output levels. However this type of competition usually does not threaten a firm's survival when markets behave in an imperfect fashion. Short run problems caused by price and quality competition will arise but eventually be overcome.

This is not however, the case with competition based on new technology. The introduction of this in an industry can entirely ruin all those firms which do not have it. Hence the struggle for new technologies is a dominant competitive variable and a failure to compete could well mean that the firm will not survive.

This argument suggests that large firms in imperfect competition are likely to devote a higher share of resources to innovation than say, firms in a perfectly competitive market and absolute monopolies. A monopolist, if assured of maintaining that position, has by definition no competition and no incentive to innovate. Firms in perfect competion have low profit margins and lack the resources to invest in new technology development. Even if they did undertake to develop a new technology, the time lag and ease of entry to the industry means their returns would quickly be competed away. Thus with an increasing number of large firms (but not monopoly firms) increasing innovation might be expected.

---

53 Carter, C. F., & Williams, B. R., *Investment in Innovation,* Oxford University Press, Oxford, 1958.

Table 21
Estimated Index of the Innovation Rate in Major Innovations per R & D Dollar*

	FIRM SIZE (total number of employees)		
Years	1-1000	1000-10,000	10,000+
1953-59	100	29.5	3.9
1960-66	64.4	14.4	2.2
1967-73	35.1	9.0	2.0

Source: *Government Policies and Factors Influencing the Innovation Capability of SME's.* Paper prepared by the OECD Secretariat and Staffgroup Strategic Studies TNO, OECD, May, 1978.

*Numbers are relative to the innovation rate for companies of 1 to 1000 employees in the 1953-59 period. This rate is assigned the value 100.

The empirical evidence in support of this proposition is mixed. Absolute levels of R & D expenditure are highly correlated with the size of a firm but the share of resources within a firm devoted to research and development is not so strongly correlated with firm size[54]. It appears that once some threshold size is reached big firms do not do relatively more R & D spending than smaller ones[55]. This is not surprising as very big firms tend to move towards monopoly behaviour and show less inclination to innovate.

Despite the evidence of concentration of R & D expenditure in large firms it is nevertheless not necessarily true that these firms account for the dominant share of invention and innovations. In the US the National Science Foundation has estimated that innovation per dollar expenditure on R & D is much higher in small firms[56]. This finding has also been supported by an OECD study and the results of it are summarized in Table 21.

---

[54] Villard, H. H., Competition, Oligopoly and Research, *Journal of Political Economy*, December 1958.

Hamberg, D., Size of Firm, Oligopoly and Research: The Evidence, *Canadian Journal of Economics & Political Science* February, 1964.

[55] Scherer, F. M., Firm Size, Market Structures, Opportunities and the Output of Patented Inventions, *American Economic Review* December 1965.

Scherer, F. M., Size of Firm, Oligopoly and Research: A Comment, *Canadian Journal of Economics & Political Science,* May/June 1965.

Hamberg, D., *ibid.*

[56] Rothwell, R. & Zegveld, W., *Some Recent Trends in Government Policy towards Innovation in Small and Medium Sized Manufacturing Enterprises,* Paper prepared for conference on Innovation Studies in the UK: the State of the Art and Directions for Future Research, 1979.

It shows the number of innovations occuring in small firms per dollar spent on R & D to be notably higher than that in larger firms for the 1953-73 period among OECD countries. However, the number of innovations may be less important than their quality and diffusion.

The reason for the higher productivity of R & D in small firms has been suggested by Abernathy and Utterbach[57]. They argue that large firms specialize in mature products where competition is primarily on the basis of incremental cost saving innovations and minor product improvements. On the other hand small and new technology based firms compete on the basis of entirely new products; performance and quality are more important than price in this form of technological competition. This behaviour is apparent in the electronics industry in the US where radical innovations have been introduced by small technologically progressive firms before being introduced later to large firms both in the United States and abroad. The new small firms, because of their non-hierarchical management structure and willingness to take risks on the basis of a highly skilled workforce, have provided the technological lead[58].

This pattern of behaviour is not as noticeable in other countries where the number of small firms is generally declining. It has been suggested that this is in part caused by the relative lack of venture capital elsewhere and by disincentives in particular nations' tax structures and other governmental policy structures[59].

Thus the influence of firm size on innovation appears to be mixed. Larger firms do undertake relatively more R & D but they appear not to be as productive at producing innovations as small technically progressive firms.

C. THE INFLUENCE OF THE GOVERNMENT

The effects of government behaviour on innovation are numerous but four factors can be singled out as being important. The *first* is the demand for innovations which the government itself expresses; the *second* is the effect of government subsidies and direct financial support for innovation; the third is the support for basic research and technical, and related educational, infrastructure in the economy;

---

57 Abernathy W. J. & Utterbach J. M., *Innovation and the Evolution of Technology in the Firm*, Harvard University Graduate School of Business, Cambridge, Mass. 1976.
58 The apparently high returns estimated for small firms may be a biased measure since it implicitly omits all those who go bankrupt or fail in some other form.
59 Rothwell R. & Zegveld W., *op.cit.*

and *finally* the influence of the government on the general economic climate.

The last of these factors has often been claimed to be the most important and the implications of the discussion in Chapter III of this paper stress the linkages between the economic climate and innovation. Any government policy package that manages to reduce inflation, increase investment and employment and restore stable economic growth will stimulate innovation. The problems which governments face in achieving these targets have not so far been overcome and until they are, innovation is bound to be sluggish.

But innovation also affects economic performance and the other factors of government influence upon innovation listed above are important in stimulating innovation. A recent study of fifty major clusters of innovations concluded that the most important factor of influence was demand[60]. A strong and clearly expressed government demand for particular innovations had the effect of decreasing risk and uncertainty by guaranteeing a future market. The more radical the innovation, the more important this influence was. The government in effect places orders with industry for a specific product or process innovation and guarantees to buy the output.

The SAPPHO research project also found that the support given by government to basic research and general technical education made a major contribution to innovation. In electronics and chemicals the universities were found to be especially important in originating major inventions and developing the necessary background technology. In nuclear power, aircraft and engine development, government-financed research laboratories were important except for the original basic physics which came from the universities. In mechanical equipment and process innovations in bulk materials, neither government nor university laboratories made any significant contribution[61].

The effect of government subsidies and direct financial support for innovation is less clear. A number of economists question the need for such support and argue that it can well induce the financing of commercially second-best projects. If an innovation is commercially worth doing, then most industrial firms either have or can raise the resources needed to carry out the innovation. Government subsidy will simply lead to inefficiency. There is some

---

60   Science Policy Research Unit, *SAPPHO Project,* University of Sussex, Falmer, Brighton. 1971.

61   *The Current International Economic Climate and Policies for Technical Innovation,* Science Policy Research Unit, Sussex, and Staffgroup Strategic Surveys, TNO, The Netherlands; November 1977.

Table 22
Deployment of Government Financed Expenditure on R & D in Selected Countries, 1975

	UK	Canada	US	France	West Germany	Japan
1. General advancement of knowledge	21.4%	25.2%	3.9%	25.3%	51.0%	55.8%
2. Agriculture and health	6.5	25.4	13.7	8.4	5.2	16.6
3. Defence	48.9	6.1	49.8	29.5	11.1	2.2
4. Civilian industry	26.8	29.5	21.3	25.8	22.3	20.0
5. Quality of life	4.7	14.7	11.2	10.1	10.3	5.9
6. Other	0	0	0	0.4	0	0
Total	100	100	100	100	100	100

Source: *Science and Technology in the New Socio-Economic Context*, OECD.

evidence to support this view. "Launching aid" for civil aviation projects in the United Kingdom has been highly unprofitable; government intervention in the French computer industry hindered the necessary adjustment towards profitable products[62].

This argument may be true for "big" science projects in the nuclear, aircraft and electronics industry. Indeed, in the UK and US these are the sectors where government support is concentrated. Canada is an exception; here government support has been spread more evenly across all sectors of industry. Mechanical engineering and paper industries are given priority, but most industries receive substantial support. In Canada support from the IDAP programme has also concentrated on firms with less than 1000 employees who received in all 57% of that programme's support. On the basis of the previous discussion about better R & D productivity in small firms this seems sensible practice although the possibility for inefficiencies still exists. A Canadian study has compared R & D projects totally funded by industry with those R & D projects partly financed by government. It noted that the latter tended to have the following properties. They were technically more ambitious, higher risk projects, involving high development costs, and resulting in higher financial loss in the case of failure. These projects had similar sales potential but were in markets with lower growth prospects[63].

It seems therefore that there are clear dangers and difficulties associated with government subsidy. Like any subsidy it can easily lead to inefficiencies, but it should not be concluded that the government need only fund basic research and skills. A case can be made for that policy only if markets were perfect but their imperfections suggest that government intervention may not be necessarily inefficient. Nevertheless, more regard to cost and market realities is needed when allocating scarce resources.

The deployment of government financed expenditure on R & D in selected countries is shown in Table 22. The most notable features are the high proportion of R & D defence spending in the United Kingdom and the United States and the high proportion of resources devoted to the general advancement of knowledge in Japan and West Germany. It seems highly likely that these latter two countries benefitted economically from the fact that the US and the UK, with whom they compete, have devoted so many resources to defence. The value of the spin-offs that result

---

62 *ibid.*
63 Science Policy Research Unit, Sussex, and Staffgroup Strategic Surveys, TNO, The Netherlands, *op.cit.*

from such a resource allocation is most unlikely to equal the value of R & D directed at more commercial objectives.

This is not to deny the importance of national security but the existence of such a high defence commitment, especially in the United Kingdom, certainly needs more investigation and questioning than it has currently received. Its opportunity cost may be extremely high in a country with so many structural economic problems.

There are various specific policies that could be pursued to achieve an increase in innovation. The research stage often begins with a basic discovery drawn from existing or recently acquired knowledge. The level of basic research performed in the economy adds to this knowledge and provides access to it. For this reason adequate levels of basic research funding must be maintained. There has been little increase in this activity since 1967 in the United Kingdom, Canada and the United States and their investment in this sphere compares unfavourably with that of their competitors. Industry will not normally adequately fund this part of the innovation process as the returns that accrue to it cannot usually be appropriated as they are shared freely across the economy. As a consequence, it is vital that government funding is maintained for basic research in universities and other public and private research establishments. The empirical evidence suggests that in both the UK and the US the government has allocated proportionately less resources to basic research over at least the last five years, and this has serious implications for the future.

This is not to argue that basic research is needed because without it basic discoveries will not be made. Rather it is that if basic research is not carried out then development in an area of knowledge, wherever that happens, may not be monitored or the significance of discoveries properly understood.

The ability to keep up with technical breakthroughs elsewhere is important if such discoveries are subsequently to be used commercially. Japan is probably the country which shows most dramatically how important this aspect of R & D can become.

Related to this argument is the evidence that there are usually long time lags between the basic research discovery and the recognition of its commercial applicability. These time lags could be made shorter if there was more contact and information flowing between universities and industry. The success to date of the modest Innovation Centres programme in the US, and similar schemes in other countries, shows the possibilities of such action.

The US centres are supported by government for five years

and, if successful, become self-sustaining. They were conceived as vehicles within universities for stimulating technological innovation and increasing entrepreneurship amongst graduate students. Each centre has a particular emphasis that derives from its institutional setting.

So far three centres have been awarded $3 million from the National Science Foundation for their operation over five years. By 1979 they had participated in the creation of 30 new ventures of which 23 had achieved sales of over $30 million. They had created 1,050 new jobs, generated $6 million in tax and evaluated 2,000 new products or ideas. Over 2,000 students have been involved. Whether similar schemes could be repeated in the UK or Canada, or extended further in the US needs investigating. Nevertheless the general point that working contacts ought to be encouraged between universities and industry is important. They offer potentially fruitful interaction between technical expertise and commercial know how and are therefore likely to lead eventually to a higher rate of innovation throughout the economy.

Applied research and development expenditure by firms is typically encouraged by governments with the use of two policy instruments: tax allowances and patent laws. When expenditure on capital equipment used in applied research and development is allowed as a corporate tax deduction through a system of general allowances and/or accelerated depreciation, it decreases tax revenues in the short run. It may of course add to tax revenues in the long run as the benefits of the research and development add to corporate income. An attempt to measure the costs and benefits of such schemes has never been made but at present benefits probably far outweigh the costs that accrue in terms of tax revenues foregone. The main aim of adopting these policies is to halt the proportionate reduction in industrial resources devoted to applied research and development and thus to contribute to halting industrial decline.

If this industrial decline is not halted, unemployment will rise and profits will fall. The tax base will then decrease resulting in a slowing of social capital formation. Policies are required then, which recognise the importance of long term research and development expenditure by firms, and which would encourage an increase in the employment of scientists and engineers in industry working on R & D. Given the heavy concentration of this activity in chemicals and electronics, such policies may encourage more diversification of national R & D into other sectors of industry where at present little occurs. This point is particularly pertinent for the United Kingdom where fewer scientists and engineers are trained and employed as a percent of the population than in the countries of their competitors. The shortage of skilled labour that has already been noted by the British-North American Committee in recent publications is also relevant to this discussion[64]. Commercialization and diffusion of innovations are often blocked or slowed down because of skill shortages; the tax provisions to encourage R & D therefore must also be accompanied by the development of more widely available technical education programmes particularly in the United Kingdom.

The second policy instrument that can be used to encourage R & D is patent law. A patent enables the appropriation of returns by the patent owner over its lifetime. Regulations about patents differ between countries and it is notable that the United States and Canada have a different system from elsewhere. In Europe a simple "first-to-file" system is followed where the first party to file is awarded the patent. If any other party has evidence to show that they actually were the first to invent and use the techniques then there is provision for personal defence. On the other hand in the US and Canada when two or more applicants seek a patent for substantially the same invention the system provides for "interference". This is a procedure to determine who first made the invention and it starts out as a proceeding in the patent office and occasionally reaches the federal courts as full-scale litigation.

These proceedings are highly technical, expensive, and time consuming and in a significant majority of cases the patent is eventually awarded to the first-to-file. The result of the "interference" procedure is simply to slow down the use of the technology covered by the patent. For these reasons it is advisable that in both the US and Canada there be a shift to the first-to-file system as it provides a personal defence for an inventor who has evidence of first invention and use but who has not filed. The main point however, is that the first-to-file system is less expensive and tends to encourage the faster adoption of techniques.

There is evidence to suggest that proposals to lengthen the life of patents will have little effect on the pace of innovation[65]. For

---

64 W. W. Winpisinger, *A Trade Union View of US Manpower Policy*, BNAC, Washington, Montreal, London, 1980.

W. Dodge, *Skilled Labour Supply Imbalance: The Canadian Experience*, BNAC, Washington, Montreal, London, 1977.

G. Eastwood, *Skilled Labour Shortages in the UK: With Particular Reference to the Engineering Industry*, BNAC, Washington, Montreal, London, 1976.

65 Schott, Kerry, The Relations Between Industrial Research & Development and Factor Demand, *Economic Journal*, March 1978 and

Taylor, C. T. & Z. A. Silberston, *The Economic Impact of the Patent System*, Cambridge University Press, Cambridge, 1973.

instance, most existing patents are not now used for the full length of their life and hence increasing the time over which they can be appropriated is unlikely to alter matters.

Other changes in the patent law in the US have recently been recommended by the Committee for Economic Development[66]. It states that patent disputes which arise should not always be dealt with in courts. Provided both parties agree, it is suggested that the dispute could be handled by arbitration. Disputes are not infrequent over commercially important patents as competitors tend to disagree with patent owners concerning the scope and true value of their inventions. As litigation procedures are expensive, often $500,000 or more per party, voluntary arbitration would be cheaper and faster.

Patent policy therefore, should move to the "first-to-file" system in Canada and the US with the implementation of changes, to permit disputes to be settled more quickly and less expensively. However, the overall effect of these adjustments to the US and Canadian patent systems is unlikely to provide a major stimulation of innovation. Patents are of importance in some industries only and in any case a favourable patenting climate does not necessarily ensure the implementation of the techniques embodied in the patents.

The schemes discussed so far to encourage innovation have been specific to R & D. They have involved encouraging basic research, contact between universities and industry, and stimulating policies to encourage applied research and development. These policy changes together would stimulate R & D; but it is only part of the innovation process, and frequently a low cost part. As a result it has been argued that broad based incentives and allowances are the most important for stimulating innovation. Neither increasing the performance of R & D nor the filing of more patents assures that commercialization and subsequent diffusion of an innovation will occur. These latter stages are best encouraged by creating a climate where expected returns on new investment are increasingly favourable. Effective market research for potential products or processes by the innovator at an early stage seems to be a vital ingredient if R & D is eventually to result in a successful innovation.

A government concerned about low industrial R & D can also introduce broad based incentives such as lower corporate taxes on profits, investment allowances to offset tax or accelerated depreciation allowances. Reducing corporate taxes does have the

---

66 Committee for Economic Development, *Stimulating Technological Progress*, Washington D.C., 1980.

considerable advantage of helping all profitable firms and leaves the decisions about how to proceed with expansion or rationalisation free of distortionary effects that can result from simply concentrating incentives on one particular factor. In theory such a tax incentive policy has much to recommend it, but in the United Kingdom the effective level of corporate taxation is already extremely low, and close to zero in many cases. Thus in the UK a decrease in corporate taxes or an increase in investment allowances is unlikely to have any immediate effect on R & D activity. In the United States and Canada on the other hand, the effective corporate tax ratio is higher and lowering tax rates or increasing investment allowances ought to encourage industrial R & D activity.

D. SUMMARY

The general economic climate has deteriorated throughout the seventies and this has had a major impact on the innovative efforts of all countries. However, the relatively poor economic performances of the United Kingdom, Canada and the United States particularly, has meant that their innovation activity has been more severely affected.

Declining profits together with increased investment costs in the three countries have also contributed to a lower priority being given to innovation as managements have had to turn their attention to survival strategies.

Relatively large firms appear to be more research intensive than small ones but their R & D expenditure has not produced as many major innovations per R & D dollar spent as in small technically progressive firms. These small firms are increasing in number in the US but not apparently in the UK and Canada.

The government influences innovation through its management of the economy, its own demand for innovations, its subsidy provisions and its direct funding of research. The latter acts as a stimulus to innovation but the major direct impact of government seems to be through its expressed demand for products. Subsidies and direct funding of industrial R & D by government can be an inefficient use of public sector resources.

IV Policy Issues

The most obvious point arising from the two preceding chapters is the interrelation between the state of the economy and innovation activity. The relatively poor economic performances of the United Kingdom, Canada and the United States is discouraging to industrial innovation and its relative decline in these three countries then contributes to further economic deterioration.

The recent economic history of the three countries has been extensively documented and comparisons made with Japan and West Germany. It is noteworthy that the productivity growth rates in Britain and North America are comparatively low and are declining faster than those of their competitors. At the same time investment per capita is also relatively low and unemployment rates are relatively high. This is particularly apparent in the United Kingdom whose current economic problems are more severe than those of other countries under consideration: The position in the United States is also of concern. The productivity slowdown there is most marked and because of the large absolute size of that economy the effects of its economic performance on the rest of the world are that much greater.

These economic factors all influence the pace and level of innovation and it is significant, but not surprising, that all the indicators of innovation suggest that the share of resources devoted to it in these three countries has declined. Their innovative efforts also compare unfavourably with those in France, and especially West Germany and Japan. The effect of this relative decline in innovation then goes on to be a contributing factor in the deteriorating economic performance of the United Kingdom, Canada and the United States. As their productivity and growth are affected so their share of trade declines, investment falls, and unemployment increases as output falters. This is the "circularity of influence" discussed earlier. The general economic climate affects innovation which itself influences economic performance.

One of the obvious consequences of this circularity of influence, is that an improvement in economic conditions would stimulate innovation. It appears too simple to conclude that if stable prices and economic growth could be achieved this would be the best stimulus for innovation that could possibly be devised. Yet this is true.

Considerable difficulty continues to be experienced in using macroeconomic policies both to control inflation and stimulate output. Coping with these difficulties is well beyond the scope of this study but it is worthwhile pointing out that macroeconomic policy must focus on aggregate supply as well as on demand management. If increased aggregate demand is not accompanied by an increase in the supply of goods and services the most likely result is rising prices. Furthermore, an increase in productivity, which would in all likelihood be associated with increased innovation, could have the dual effect of increasing the output of goods and services and decreasing prices. On the basis of the evidence examined earlier it seems imperative that innovation be encouraged further in the United Kingdom, Canada and the United States. Indeed such a policy is vital if the industries in these countries are to recover from their currently depressed levels and compete effectively in world markets.

However, stimulating innovation on its own would be misguided because of the circularity between economic performance and innovation. It follows that policies to encourage innovation should be part of a more complete policy package to stimulate economic recovery. This comprehensive approach is important if policy is to be efficient and successful. Any attempt simply to stimulate innovation on its own is unlikely to succeed. Industrial innovation occurs along with new investment and the latter takes place only if profitable returns are expected. Hence innovation should be encouraged, but as part of a comprehensive economic policy which is also directed towards the stimulation of investment and industrial recovery.

The other major point that must be emphasised which arises from the discussion in Chapter II is the uneven pattern of research and development across industry. Most privately funded R & D in Britain and North America is concentrated in electronics and chemicals. This means that when we talk of a relative decline in industrial innovation we are really emphasising a relative decline of it in these two industries.

This concentration of private industrial R & D in chemicals and electronics is also apparent in other countries, including West Germany and Japan; but R & D activity is more evenly distributed across industries in these countries. This raises the immediate question of what would be the result of it being more evenly spread across industries in the UK, Canada and the US? For instance, would it raise profitability in those industries and overall? There is unfortunately no clearcut answer to this question but the evidence in Chapter I suggests that innovative activity in both Britain and the United States would benefit from more research and development activity, particularly in neglected sectors of industry.

With this in mind the discussion in this chapter now turns to a consideration of policies that would encourage R & D and innovation. The specific mechanics of particular policies are not discussed, because these must differ in each country, but the general type of policies that can help are considered. Policies specifically designed to encourage innovation are required because this activity embodies more uncertainty within industry than virtually any other. The expected returns from any particular R & D programme may be high but the likely variance is also high; for this reason extra help may be required. This is especially important at this time, when the economic outlook is so uncertain—a situation which inhibits innovation activity further.

It would also be helpful if investment allowances for tax purposes did not differentiate between buildings and plant and equipment. If investment allowances or accelerated depreciation are allowed only on machinery and equipment, then this type of investment will be favoured because of this distortion.

The government can also reduce the uncertainty attached to the innovation process through its role as a customer. Its requirements can be formed to stimulate innovation as its orders are frequently large and payment is certain. For instance, the defence demands of the US and UK governments encourage innovations in defence-related activities such as aerospace but encouragement to innovate must be directed to areas where economic benefits may be expected to exceed economic costs. This is particularly important in the UK where a great deal of government funded innovation is defence oriented and generally economic performance is relatively very poor.

Several factors that are likely to inhibit innovation are worth examining. Where a shortage of venture capital occurs, particularly for small firms, credit guarantee schemes can be devised or further encouraged perhaps along the lines of the Canadian Enterprise Development Programme. Under this scheme firms can obtain loan guarantees on venture capital for 90% of their borrowings at an insurance cost of 1% per annum.

Finally, if the encouragement of industrial research and development in the United States, Canada and the United Kingdom is disregarded, then the chances of successful commercial innovations in both products and processes are further reduced. To maintain their economic base in the face of acute competition from both developed and newly industrializing countries, this matter is of vital importance to them. Because innovative activity is slow and often uncertain in its outcome, it tends to be relegated to a low position in national priotities; yet it is becoming the only comparative advantage the developed countries have. Innovation is therefore of vital concern in the industries of Britain and North America.

Members of the British-North American Committee

Chairmen
SIR ALASTAIR DOWN
Chairman,
Burmah Oil Company,
Swindon, Wiltshire

WILLIAM WEARLY
Chairman, Executive Committee,
Ingersoll-Rand Company,
Woodcliff Lake, New Jersey

Vice Chairman
GEORGE SHULTZ
Vice Chairman,
Bechtel Group of Companies,
San Francisco, California

Chairman, Executive Committee
WILLIAM I. M. TURNER, JR.
President and Chief Executive Officer,
Consolidated-Bathurst Inc.,
Montreal, Quebec

Members
R. W. ADAM
A Managing Director,
The British Petroleum Company Limited,
London

WILLIAM M. AGEE
Chairman and Chief Executive Officer,
The Bendix Corporation, Southfield,
Michigan

J. A. ARMSTRONG
Chairman and Chief Executive Officer,
Imperial Oil Limited, Toronto, Ontario

CHARLES F. BAIRD
Chairman and Chief Executive Officer,
INCO Limited, Toronto, Ontario

JOSEPH E. BAIRD
Pacific Palisades, California

ROBERT A. BANDEEN
President and Chief Executive Officer,
Canadian National, Montreal, Quebec

W. G. BARRETT
General Manager,
Midland Bank Limited, International Division,
London

SIR DONALD BARRON
Trustee,
The Joseph Rowntree Memorial Trust, York,
Yorkshire

CARL E. BEIGIE
President,
C. D. Howe Institute, Montreal, Quebec

MICHEL BELANGER
President and Chief Executive Officer,
National Bank of Canada, Montreal, Quebec

C. FRED BERGSTEN
Senior Associate,
Carnegie Endowment for International Peace,
Washington, D.C.

CARROL D. BOLEN
President,
Illinois-Wisconsin Division, Pioneer Hi-Bred
International, Inc., Princeton, Illinois

JOHN F. BOOKOUT
President and Chief Executive Officer,
Shell Oil Company, Houston, Texas

FRANK BORMAN
Chairman, President and Chief Executive
Officer,
Eastern Airlines, Miami, Florida

THORNTON F. BRADSHAW
President,
Atlantic Richfield Company, Los Angeles,
California

JAMES W. BURNS
President,
Power Corporation of Canada Ltd., Montreal,
Quebec

SIR GEORGE BURTON
Chairman,
Fisons Limited, London

SIR RICHARD BUTLER
President,
National Farmers' Union, London

VISCOUNT CALDECOTE
Chairman, Delta Metal Company and
Chairman, Finance for Industry, London

SIR CHARLES CARTER
Chairman of Research and Management
Committee, Policy Studies Institute, London

SILAS S. CATHCART
Chairman and Chief Executive Officer,
Illinois Tool Works, Inc., Chicago, Illinois

HAROLD VAN B. CLEVELAND
Vice President,
Citibank, N.A., New York, N.Y.

DONALD M. COX
Director and Senior Vice President,
Exxon Corporation, New York, N.Y.

Committee Members

FRANK J. CUMMISKEY
IBM Vice President and President,
General Business Group/International,
IBM Corporation, White Plains, New York

JAMES W. DAVANT
Chairman of the Board,
Paine Webber Incorporated, New York, N. Y.

RALPH P. DAVIDSON
Chairman,
Time Incorporated, New York, N.Y.

DIRK DE BRUYNE
Managing Director,
Royal Dutch/Shell Group of Companies,
London

A. H. A. DIBBS
Deputy Chairman,
National Westminster Bank Limited, London

SIR RICHARD DOBSON
Richmond, Surrey

WILLIAM DODGE
Ottawa, Ontario

WILLIAM H. DONALDSON
Chairman and Chief Executive,
Donaldson Enterprises Inc., New York, N.Y.

PETER P. DONIS
Executive Vice President,
Caterpillar Tractor Company, Peoria, Illinois

GEOFFREY DRAIN
General Secretary,
National Association of Local Government Officers, London

JOHN DU CANE
Chairman and Chief Executive,
Selection Trust Limited, London

TERRY DUFFY
President,
Amalgamated Union of Engineering Workers,
London

GERRY EASTWOOD
General Secretary,
Association of Patternmakers and Allied Craftsmen, London

HARRY E. EKBLOM
Chairman and Chief Executive Officer,
European American Bancorp, New York, N.Y.

MOSS EVANS
General Secretary,
Transport and General Workers' Union,
London

J. K. FINLAYSON
President,
The Royal Bank of Canada, Toronto, Ontario

GLENN FLATEN
President,
Canadian Federation of Agriculture, Regina, Saskatchewan

SIR ALASTAIR FRAME
Chief Executive,
Rio-Tinto Zinc Corporation, London

RICHARD W. FOXEN
Corporate Vice President-International,
Rockwell International Corp., Pittsburgh, Pennsylvania

ROBERT R. FREDERICK
Executive Vice President,
International Sector,
General Electric Company, Fairfield, Connecticut

THEODORE GEIGER
Distinguished Research Professor of Intersocietal Relations School of Foreign Service, Georgetown University,
Washington, D.C.

GWAIN GILLESPIE
Senior Vice President-Finance & Administration,
Heublein Inc., Farmington, Connecticut

MALCOLM GLENN
Executive Vice President,
Reed Holdings, Incorporated,
Rickmansworth, Herts.

GEORGE GOYDER
British Secretary,
BNAC, Sudbury, Suffolk

JOHN H. HALE
Executive Vice President,
Alcan Aluminium Limited, Montreal, Quebec

HON. HENRY HANKEY
Westerham, Kent

AUGUSTIN S. HART, JR.
Director,
Quaker Oats Company, Chicago, Illinois

FRED L. HARTLEY
Chairman and President,
Union Oil Company of California,
Los Angeles, California

G. R. HEFFERNAN
President,
Co-Steel International Ltd., Whitby, Ontario

HENRY J. HEINZ II
Chairman of the Board,
H. J. Heinz Company, Pittsburg, Pennsylvania

ROBERT HENDERSON
Chairman, Kleinwort Benson Ltd., London

*TREVOR HOLDSWORTH
Chairman,
Guest, Keen & Nettlefolds Ltd., London

HENDRIK S. HOUTHAKKER
Professor of Economics,
Harvard University, Cambridge,
Massachusetts

TOM JACKSON
General Secretary,
Union of Communication Workers, London

DONALD P. JACOBS
Dean,
J. L. Kellogg Graduate School of
Management, Northwestern University,
Evanston, Illinois

JOHN V. JAMES
Chairman of the Board, President and Chief
Executive Officer,
Dresser Industries, Inc., Dallas, Texas

GEORGE S. JOHNSTON
President,
Scudder, Stevens & Clark, New York, N.Y.

JOSEPH D. KEENAN
President,
Union Label and Service Trades Department,
AFL-CIO, Washington, D.C.

TOM KILLEFER
Chairman of the Board and Chief Executive
Officer, United States Trust Company of New
York, New York, N.Y.

CURTIS M. KLAERNER
President and Chief Operating Officer,
Commonwealth Oil Refining Company,
San Antonio, Texas

H. U. A. LAMBERT
Chairman,
Barclays Bank International Ltd., London

HERBERT H. LANK
Honorary Director,
Du Pont Canada Inc., Montreal, Quebec

WILLIAM A. LIFFERS
Vice Chairman,
American Cyanamid Company, Wayne, New
Jersey

FRANKLIN A. LINDSAY
Chairman,
Itek Corporation, Lexington, Massachusetts

SIR PETER MACADAM
Chairman,
B.A.T. Industries Ltd., London

RAY W. MACDONALD
Honorary Chairman,
Burroughs Corporation, Stuart, Florida

IAN MacGREGOR
Honorary Chairman,
AMAX Inc., Greenwich, Connecticut

CARGILL MacMILLAN, JR.
Senior Vice President,
Cargill Inc., Minneapolis, Minnesota

JOHN D. MACOMBER
Chairman,
Celanese Corporation, New York, N.Y.

J. P. MANN
Deputy Chairman,
United Biscuits (Holdings) Ltd., Isleworth,
Middlesex

WILLIAM A. MARQUARD
Chairman, President and Chief Executive
Officer,
American Standard Inc., New York, N.Y.

A. B. MARSHALL
Chairman, Bestobell Ltd., London

DENNIS McDERMOTT
President,
Canadian Labour Congress, Ottawa, Ontario

WILLIAM J. McDONOUGH
Chairman, Asset and Liability Management
Committee,
The First National Bank of Chicago, Chicago,
Illinois

DONALD E. MEADS
Chairman and President,
Carver Associates, Plymouth Meeting,
Pennsylvania

SIR PATRICK MEANEY
Group Managing Director,
Thomas Tilling Limited, London

C. J. MEDBERRY III
Chairman of the Board,
BankAmerica Corporation and Bank of
America NT&SA, Los Angeles, California

SIR PETER MENZIES
Welwyn, Hertfordshire

---

*Became a member of the Committee after the statement was circulated for signature.

Committee Members

JOHN MILLER
Vice Chairman, and Acting President,
National Planning Association,
Washington, D.C.

DEREK F. MITCHELL
Chairman and Chief Executive Officer,
BP Canada Limited, Toronto, Ontario

JOSEPH P. MONGE
Chief Executive Officer,
California Life Corporation, Los Angeles,
California

DONALD R. MONTGOMERY
Secretary-Treasurer,
Canadian Labour Congress, Ottawa, Ontario

ALLEN E. MURRAY
President of Marketing and Refining Division,
Mobil Oil Corporation, New York, N.Y.

KENNETH D. NADEN
President,
National Council of Farmer Cooperatives,
Washington, D.C.

CONOR CRUISE O'BRIEN
Director,
Observer Newspaper Company, Ltd., London

WILLIAM S. OGDEN
Vice Chairman,
The Chase Manhattan Bank, N.A., New York,
N.Y.

PAUL PARE
Chairman and Chief Executive Officer,
Imasco Ltd., Montreal, Quebec

PAUL L. PARKER
Executive Vice President,
General Mills, Inc., Minneapolis, Minnesota

BROUGHTON PIPKIN
Stow-on-the-Wold, Glouc.

GEORGE J. POULIN
General Vice President,
International Association of Machinists &
Aerospace Workers, Washington, D.C.

SIR RICHARD POWELL
Hill Samuel Group Ltd., London

ALFRED POWIS
Chairman and President,
Noranda Mines Limited, Toronto, Ontario

J. G. PRENTICE
Chairman of the Board,
Canadian Forest Products Ltd., Vancouver,
British Columbia

PAUL E. PRICE
Senior Vice President-Finance,
Quaker Oats Company, Chicago, Illinois

LOUIS PUTZE
Consultant,
Rockwell International, Corp., Pittsburgh,
Pennsylvania

MERLE RAWSON
Chairman and Chief Executive Officer,
The Hoover Company, North Canton, Ohio

CARL E. REICHARDT
President and Director,
Wells Fargo Bank, San Francisco, California

BEN ROBERTS
Professor of Industrial Relations,
London School of Economics, London

HAROLD B. ROSE
Group Economic Advisor,
Barclays Bank Limited, London

DAVID SAINSBURY
Director of Finance,
J. Sainsbury Ltd., London

WILLIAM SALOMON
Limited Partner and Honorary Member of the
Executive Committee,
Salomon Brothers, New York, N.Y.

A.C.I. SAMUEL
Handcross, Sussex

HOWARD SAMUEL
President,
Industrial Union Department, AFL-CIO,
Washington, D.C.

NATHANIEL SAMUELS
Chairman, Advisory Board Lehman Brothers
Kuhn Leob Inc., and
Chairman, Olivetti Corporation New York,
N.Y.

SIR FRANCIS SANDILANDS
Chairman,
Commercial Union Assurance Company, Ltd.,
London

HON. MAURICE SAUVE
Executive Vice President, Administrative and
Public Affairs,
Consolidated Bathurst Inc., Montreal, Quebec

PETER F. SCOTT
President,
Provincial Insurance Company, Ltd., Kendal,
Westmoreland

ROBERT C. SEAMANS, JR.
Massachusetts Institute of Technology,
Cambridge, Massachusetts

LORD SEEBOHM
Dedham, Essex

THE EARL OF SELKIRK
President,
Royal Central Asian Society, London

JACOB SHEINKMAN
Secretary-Treasurer,
Amalgmated Clothing & Textile Workers' Union, New York, N.Y.

LORD SHERFIELD
Chairman,
Raytheon Europe International Company, London

R. MICHAEL SHIELDS
Managing Director,
Associated Newspapers Group Ltd., London

GEORGE L. SHINN
Chairman and Chief Executive Officer,
The First Boston Corporation, New York, N.Y.

WILLIAM E. SIMON
Blyth, Eastman, Paine, Webber, New York, N.Y.

GORDON R. SIMPSON
Chairman,
General Accident Fire and Life Assurance Corporation Ltd., Perth, Scotland

SIR ROY SISSON
Chairman,
Smiths Industries Limited, London

ARTHUR J. R. SMITH
Consultant, Washington, D.C.

SIR LESLIE SMITH
Chairman, BOC International, London

LAUREN K. SOTH
Journalist, West Des Moines, Iowa

E. NORMAN STAUB
Chairman and Chief Executive Officer,
The Northern Trust Company, Chicago, Illinois

RALPH I. STRAUS
New York, N.Y.

SIR ROBERT TAYLOR
Deputy Chairman,
Standard Chartered Bank Ltd., London

J. C. TURNER
General President,
International Union of Operating Engineers, AFL-CIO, Washington, D.C.

JOHN W. TUTHILL
President,
The Salzburg Seminar, Washington, D.C.

W. O. TWAITS
Toronto, Ontario

MARTHA REDFIELD WALLACE
Director,
The Henry Luce Foundation Inc., New York, N.Y.

GLENN E. WATTS
President,
Communications Workers of America, AFL-CIO, Washington, D.C.

VISCOUNT WEIR
Vice Chairman,
The Weir Group Limited, Cathcart, Scotland

FREDERICK B. WHITTEMORE
Managing Director,
Morgan Stanley & Co. Incorporated, New York, N.Y.

SIR ERNEST WOODROOFE
Former Chairman,
Unilever Ltd., Guildford, Surrey

CHARLES WOOTTON
Senior Director, Foreign and Domestic Policy Analysis & Planning,
Gulf Oil Corporation, Pittsburgh, Pennsylvania

Sponsoring Organisations

The British-North American Research Association was inaugurated in December 1969. Its primary purpose is to sponsor research on British-North American economic relations in association with the British-North American Committee. Publications of the British-North American Research Association as well as publications of the British-North American Committee are available at the Association's office, 1 Gough Square, London EC4A 3DE (Tel. 01-353-6371). The Association is recognised as a charity and is governed by a Council under the chairmanship of Sir Alastair Down.

NPA is an independent, private, nonprofit, nonpolitical organisation that carries on research and policy formulation in the public interest. NPA was founded during the Great Depression of the 1930s when conflicts among the major economic groups—business, labour, agriculture—threatened to paralyse national decision making on the critical issues confronting American society. It is dedicated to the task of getting these diverse groups to work together to narrow areas of controversy and broaden areas of agreement and to provide, for specific problems, concrete programmes for action, planned in the best traditions of a functioning democracy. Such democratic planning, NPA believes, involves the development of effective policies and programmes not only by official agencies but also through the independent initiative and cooperation of the main private-sector groups concerned. And, to preserve and strengthen American political and economic democracy, the necessary government actions have to be consistent with, and stimulate the support of, a dynamic private sector.

NPA brings together influential and knowledgeable leaders from business, labour, agriculture, and the applied and academic professions to serve on policy committees. These committees identify emerging problems confronting the nation at home and abroad and seek to develop and agree upon policies and programmes for coping with them. The research and writing for these committees are provided by NPA's professional staff and, as required, by outside experts.

In addition, NPA's professional staff undertakes research designed to provide data and ideas for policy makers and planners in government and the private sector. These activities include the preparation on a regular basis of economic and demographic projections for the national economy, regions, states, metropolitan areas, and counties; research on national goals and priorities, productivity and economic growth, welfare and dependency problems, inflation, employment and manpower needs, energy and environmental questions, and other economic and social problems confronting American society; and analyses and forecasts of changing domestic and international realities and their implications for US policies. In developing its staff capabilities, NPA has increasingly emphasised two related qualifications.

First is the development of the interdisciplinary knowledge required to understand the complex nature of many real-life problems. Second is the ability to bridge the gap between theoretical or highly technical research and the practical needs of policy makers and planners in government and the private sector.

NPA publications, including those of the British-North American Committee, can be obtained from the Association's office, 1606 New Hampshire Ave., N.W., Washington, D.C. 20009 (Tel. 202-265-7685).

The C. D. Howe Institute is a private, nonpolitical, nonprofit organisation founded in January 1973 by the merger of the C. D. Howe Memorial Foundation and the Private Planning Association of Canada to undertake research into Canadian economic policy issues with emphasis on fiscal, monetary and international trade policy.

C. D. Howe continues the activities of the PPAC. These include the work of three established committees, composed of agricultural, business, educational, labour, and professional leaders. The committees are the Canadian Economic Policy Committee, which since 1961 has been concentrating on Canadian economic issues; the Canadian-American Committee, which has dealt with relations between Canada and the United States since 1957 and is jointly sponsored by the NPA in Washington and C. D. Howe; and the British-North American Committee, formed in 1969 and sponsored jointly by the British-North American Research Association in London, NPA and C. D. Howe. Each of the three committees meets twice a year to consider important current issues and to sponsor and review studies that contribute to a better public understanding of such issues.

In addition to taking over the publications of the three PPAC committees, C. D. Howe releases the work of its staff, and occasionally of outside authors, in four other publications: *Observations* a number of which are published each year; *Policy Review and Outlook*, published annually; *Special Studies*, to provide detailed analysis of major policy issues; and *Commentaries*, to give wide circulation to the views of experts on issues of current Canadian interest.

C. D. Howe publications, including those of the British-North American Committee, are available from the Institute's offices, Suite 2064, 1155 Metcalfe Street, Montreal, Quebec H3B 2X7 (Tel. 514-879-1254).